Writing
Your
Life Story

Writing
Your
Life Story

A STEP-BY-STEP GUIDE TO WRITING YOUR AUTOBIOGRAPHY

NANCY SMITH

PIATKUS

DEDICATION

This book is dedicated to all those students who allowed me
to share something of the pain, pleasures and immense
richness of their lives, some of whom are represented in these
pages. And, as always, to my dear children, Jan, Richard
and Mark, who unfailingly enrich *my* life.

First published in Great Britain in 1993 by
Judy Piatkus (Publishers) Ltd of
5 Windmill Street, London W1

**The moral right of the author
has been asserted**

*A catalogue record for this book is available
from the British Library*

ISBN 0-7499-1253-7

Set in Compugraphic Baskerville by
Action Typesetting, Gloucester
Printed and bound in Great Britain by
Biddles Ltd, Guildford and King's Lynn

Contents

Contents

Acknowledgements

I wish to thank all those who have so generously allowed me to reproduce in this book extracts from their autobiographies. These have greatly added, I am sure, both to its depth and interest. I also thank Anne Matthews for allowing me to use her article in the Revision section, Paula Atkins for permission to reprint an edited version of her article on self-publishing, which had previously appeared in The Society of Authors' Publication, *The Author*, and Margaret Finch for permission to reprint *St Joe, Martyr*. And, above all, of course, Winifred Foley for her Introduction. She, surely, must be an inspiration to everyone considering writing up their life story.

The author wishes to thank the following relevant authors, agents and publishers for permission to include extracts from various copyright material. Rogers, Coleridge & White Ltd for *An Immaculate Mistake* by Paul Bailey, originally published by Bloomsbury; Macmillan Publishing Company, New York, for *They Must Have Seen Me Coming* by Louise Brindley, originally published by Cassell; SPCK for *Not Quite Heaven* by Brenda Courtie; Transworld Publishers Limited for *Not Without My Daughter* by Betty Mahmoody with William Hoffer · 1987, published by Corgi Books;

Peters Fraser & Dunlop for *Diana's Story* by Deric Longden, published by Corgi Books; Andre Deutsch Ltd for *The Year of the Cornflake* by Faith Addis; Random House UK Limited for *Twopence to Cross the Mersey* by Helen Forrester; Transworld Publishers Limited for *The Past is Myself* by Christabel Bielenberg, 1984, published by Corgi Books; Faber and Faber Ltd for *Hovel in the Hills* by Elizabeth West; Douglas McLean for *A Child in the Forest* by Winifred Foley, originally published by the BBC; *A World Apart* by Daphne Rae, Lutterworth Press.

Foreword

Reading a copy of *The Countryman* as I dawdled over my midday snack, some years ago, I was reminded of my own country childhood in the Forest of Dean. Out of the blue, came the idea to write a little episode of it and send it to the editor. My elation was indescribable when I received a letter of acceptance.

Over the next couple of months, I sent two more, earning myself more fees. The family began to sit up and take notice. Fancy, poor old Mum, who had left a village school at fourteen and couldn't understand algebra, or anything about nouns and verbs to help them with their homework, was getting into print! One thing led to another and, eventually, *A Child in the Forest* was published.

It is a fact that, like our fingerprints, every human life is uniquely individual. Guided and aided from helpless babyhood to independence, we are then kept occupied in mind and body getting on with the business of living, gathering a storehouse of memories along the way.

Sooner or later comes a time to take stock and marvel at all the joys and heartaches we have experienced and the knowledge we have garnered. Often, there comes an almost irresistible urge to share the story of our lives with others, a kind of repayment and exorcism in one. There are many reasons to encourage us to do so. Just putting it down in writing can be therapeutic when the traumas of life have given us a sort of emotional indigestion. The effort is a challenge for the mind and the least it can achieve is a valuable script to leave for the future generations of our family. How often do *we* long to know more about the lives of our ancestors? Many autobiographies have made valuable contributions to the annals of social history. Occasionally, they bring fame and recognition. But, like all skills, even with a natural 'bent', advice and guidance from the experts can be very helpful.

To start writing needs little outlay – a fat, lined exercise book, a couple of biros, some of your spare time – and a book of advice.

It worked for me and for many others – and just having a try is a kind of achievement in itself. Good luck to those who do.

Winifred Foley
AUTHOR OF *A Child in the Forest*

Introduction

'Somehow I had to send myself back, with words as catalysts, to open the memories out and see what they had to offer.'

Ray Bradbury, *Dandelion Wine*

Have you thought about writing your life story but felt it was too enormous a task with so many memories jumbled together in your mind? Or have you, perhaps, wanted to try your hand at creative writing, generally, and wondered if a good place to start would be with short autobiographical pieces? If the answer to either, or both, of these questions is 'yes', then take heart – because this book is designed especially for *you*.

Having taught creative writing for many years, one thing I have discovered above all else is the infinite variety and richness of people's lives and that sticking to the maxim 'Write about what you know' results in the most fascinating tales. But, to make them also *saleable* and a pleasure for others to read, it is necessary to learn a few 'tricks of the trade', to employ fictional techniques to add colour and texture and create the tension and suspense that will persuade your reader to keep turning the pages.

Time and again, in my classes, I have found that students unwittingly leave out those vital 'brush strokes', the tiny enhancing details so clear in their own minds that they forget others don't see them, too. Or they omit incidents and episodes, believing no one else will want to hear them.

1

A student of mine once wrote of a picnic on the plains of India when she was a child, earlier this century. Discussing it in class, she casually mentioned, almost as an afterthought, that, while they were eating, a vulture had descended and snatched a sandwich out of her hand. With one voice, we all shouted: 'Put it in!' To her, in that time and place, vultures were commonplace: to the rest of us, the incident made her account all the more extraordinary.

Not all of us will want to tell our entire life story, of course. Nor do you have to have reached retirement age to write an autobiography. How old you are is irrelevant because anyone with an unusual episode to relate will find a ready audience, as did Lucy Irving with *Castaway*, her account of a year spent on a deserted island off the coast of Australia. Have you done something equally exciting – back-packing over Europe, perhaps, or to India or Nepal, seeking spiritual enlightenment? If so, why not write about it?

It may be that one particular section of your life, a specific period or just a certain episode, is especially memorable in some way, whether traumatic, dramatic, happy or sad. Perhaps you had set yourself a goal, large or small, and want to describe how you reached it. Perhaps something unexpected happened which changed your life, irrevocably, and which you think might interest others.

Putting down on paper a painful part of your life can be extremely therapeutic, often exorcising a ghost that has haunted you for too long. (Indeed, holding on to our memories can sometimes stop us from getting on with living.) It can help rid ourselves of guilt – of the 'if only I'd never' or 'where did I go wrong?' syndrome. Looking back, too, at some of the stupid, plain crazy or odd things you've done, or at least viewing them thus in retrospect and then making gentle fun of yourself, is likely to make others smile as well as allowing you to see them in perspective.

Short pieces such as these are frequently sought in magazines under various headings but coming within the generic label of 'personal experience'. They may be the humorous 'Life's Like That' kind or the more serious Self-Help ('How I overcame agoraphobia' or 'How I learned to cope with crippling shyness', for instance). Others might be 'I Was There' or 'It Happened to Me' or 'The Decision of a Lifetime', and so on. Newspapers, both national and regional, occasionally carry pieces like this from freelance contributors, *if they are well-enough written*. That is the secret, of course. They must be told vividly enough to hold the reader's attention. They must be told with sincerity, with understanding, with compassion and, where appropriate, with humour. If they are not, no editor will want them.

Thus, whether you wish to write your entire life story solely for your family and friends, starting with your birth and bringing it up to the present day, or just a part of it; whether or not you intend trying to interest a publisher in it, I believe my book will be of help.

Whenever we set out on a journey of any kind (and writing is a kind of journey), it is sensible to take along a map to avoid getting lost. This book evolved from trying to keep students, committing their lives to paper, from straying off their chosen path. Together, we discovered the problems involved and found ways of overcoming them until, eventually, I devised a method which I believe, if followed, will make your life story one which will hold a reader's interest until the end.

Neither I, nor anyone else, can guarantee success on whatever scale. Nor can I give you the necessary desire and willpower to sit down and write for many hours. I can only provide, by means of this book, some guidance as to the possible routes to follow. Hopefully, too, I will have been able to offer some inspiration and encouragement to keep on writing during those times when you wonder if you will ever finish it and if anyone will want to read it when you do.

So, tell the story of how it was for *you*. Tell it vividly, adding those touches of colour, those small details that will evoke another age, a time perhaps long gone, for those who can hardly imagine what life was like, then. Tell it for all those coming after you, whether family and friends or society in general, because, in part, you will be also compiling a social history. But, above all, tell it for yourself. Make a statement to the world at large: I lived and loved, thought and worked. I'm not perfect. I made mistakes but I have accepted myself. I may not be anybody important – *but I matter!*

HOW TO USE THIS BOOK

Because the purpose of this book is to offer both encouragement and practical help to those who feel they would like to put their life story down on paper, and to make it a less fearful task than it might at first appear, I have divided it into separate sections. These are arranged in a logical sequence, taking you step by step through the various aspects of the entire project, but they may be read separately, if you prefer.

Firstly, though, we will Take a Fresh Look at the Past to reawaken memories, before turning to:

Section 1 shows how to plan your book (essential if it is to be a coherent read and not a confusing jumble of memories), how to select and organise your material and structure individual chapters. Advice is offered on developing a good writing style (finding your own 'voice', as it is sometimes called). Finally, the importance of beginnings and endings, both of chapters and the book as a whole, is discussed and illustrated with examples from published autobiographies.

Section 2 demonstrates how to make your story more colourful and entertaining, and thus an interesting and entertaining read, by using those techniques employed by all successful fiction writers.

Section 3 tells how to write up separate episodes of your life which you may then, if you wish, try to sell to newspapers or magazines in the form of feature articles. In order to make the larger project seem more manageable, to help you gain confidence in your writing ability and 'test the water', initially, by producing short pieces, you may like to study this section, first.

Section 4 suggests ways of taking your life story a step further, if you wish, in the form of an autobiographical novel, perhaps, or writing up your family history. Or you might think of recording other people's stories, those of family members or neighbours, maybe, so that these will not be lost to posterity.

Section 5 deals with the practical aspects of writing which you also need to consider. This includes the importance of correct grammar and spelling (mentioning a few of the main errors), the right way to present your MS (manuscript)/typescript to an editor, matters of copyright and libel and so on.

Section 6 contains several pieces of autobiographical writing which illustrate something of the wide variety of people's lives. A few of these have already appeared in print while the authors of others are still seeking publication.

By the time you have read to the end, however, you should have been able to draw a map of your own particular journey through life and begun to put at least some of it on to paper. You will also have reassured yourself that it isn't so difficult after all. And, using this book as a guide, it really isn't.

TAKE A FRESH LOOK AT THE PAST

> '*The future is nothing, but the past is myself, my own history, the seed of my present thoughts, the mould of my present disposition.*'
>
> R.L. Stevenson

When you first thought of writing your autobiography, either whole or in part, you probably began asking yourself the following questions: why *my* life story? Who would want to read about me? Am I being egotistical in even thinking about putting it down on paper? Indeed, why do I want to write it and what audience do I hope to reach? Then, almost immediately, the more practical ones: how do I start the actual writing because I've never done anything like this before? Where do I begin – from the day I was born or at some point later? What do I include and what should I leave out?

These are all reasonable questions to ask, and answer, before committing yourself to the many hours of hard (though, surely, absorbing?) work necessary to produce even a short book. There is the expense to be considered, too, because, while the creative part can be handwritten, if it is to appear in print in any form, it will need to be typed and, if you can't do it yourself, you may have to pay someone else. But let us take each point, one by one.

Why YOUR Life Story?

Well, first of all, as Winifred Foley so aptly said, it is as unique as your fingerprints. No one else in the entire world has had exactly the same experiences as yourself. And, however similar they seem, their effect would have been quite different. Next, who would want to read about you? Your family and friends certainly would. They would be fascinated to learn more about someone they probably thought they already knew inside out, to understand you better, to find out what makes you tick. And, if you can write it in a warm, lively, entertaining style, it may be that others, complete strangers, would read your story with enjoyment, too.

At this point, I want to refute the generally-believed notion that publishers are only interested in the lives of the famous (or infamous!). First and foremost, they are looking for books that will *sell*, no matter who has written them. That does not mean they are waiting with open arms to be deluged with autobiographies by all and sundry – they are not –

and the odds against achieving that sort of success are high. None the less, others, no better known that yourself at the beginning, have done it – so it is not impossible.

Is it egotistical to want to share your life experiences with others? The answer to that is an unequivocal 'No'. As Somerset Maugham said in *The Summing Up*: 'I must write as though I were a person of importance; and indeed I am – to myself.'

I can truthfully say that, in my creative writing classes and courses, no work has given greater pleasure, been listened to more avidly, than that which has been autobiographical in content. And much of it was relating a social history that has vanished for ever which, if not recorded for posterity by those who actually lived through it, may never be fully understood by future generations.

Lastly, why are you writing it and what audience do you hope to reach? Well, there is the undoubted therapeutic value in putting down on paper some of the traumas and difficulties you have encountered throughout your life. (Writers of fiction often find this, too. In fact, John Mortimer once said in a TV interview that writing provides a catharsis for when things are awful and go wrong in life.) It is also an important way in which to validate your life, to banish the fear of annihilation of self which the psychologist, Dorothy Rowe, suggests we fear more than death itself. And not least, in so doing, to offer hope and courage to others who have suffered, or are suffering, some of the same problems as yourself and which you have overcome, battle-scarred, perhaps, but victorious.

Maybe, too, there are areas where you have found it difficult or impossible to communicate with those closest to you. Putting some things into writing is often easier than actually saying them out loud and this could lift a tremendous burden from your shoulders. Now, at last, they will perhaps understand – and forgive. Edna O'Brien, asked if she felt that writing was a way of explaining oneself, of making up for the failure to communicate fully in ordinary life, replied by paraphrasing Beckett, saying that we write in order to say the things we can't say and that it is an attempt to explain things and put them right.

As for your intended audience, whether it be the private one of your family and friends or you hope for a wider one through publication, not even your nearest and dearest are likely to do more than skim through it unless it makes an interesting and entertaining read. Thus, given that there is nothing wrong with wanting to write about your life, how do you set about it?

How Do I Start?

The best way, first of all, is to take a fresh look at the past, bearing in mind that the task of any autobiography is not only to inform, it is also to illuminate and inspire, to attest to our survival and, in so doing, move our readers to laughter or tears or shivers of horror.

After that, you will need to *plan* your book, to decide what to include and what to leave out, whether or not to draw upon your entire life or to record only a particular period which might be of exceptional interest not only to yourself but also to others. You may feel, for instance, that you want to start by introducing your parents or even your grandparents, setting the scene before your own birth and then proceeding chronologically. Or you might choose to divide it by using specific headings such as Early Child-hood; Schooldays; Family; Illnesses; Holidays and so on. You may decide, too, as memories unfold, that you prefer not to tell it 'warts and all' but to leave out the not-so-pleasant bits. Indeed, that particular decision is probably the biggest you will have to make when embarking upon the project.

But back to reminiscing – and is there anyone who does not like to indulge in this, at times? It is said that, if any two people are asked to recollect the same event, their versions will differ considerably. And so, when writing our life story, we will be portraying the truth as *we* see it. Thus, it is *our* truth, *our* story.

Think back to any events or periods that stand out clearly in your memory and try to recall their highlights. They will undoubtedly include major ones such as your first job, your wedding day, the birth of your first child, and so on. But don't forget some of those simpler moments of joy or pain or sorrow – the Sunday afternoon walks in spring with a favourite aunt; the day you had to have your faithful old dog put down; saying goodbye to a dear friend, knowing you would never see him or her again. All these will strike chords with your readers.

Maybe some of these are linked in some way with world-wide occasions which will add interest to others. For instance, my beloved Jack Russell terrier Muff produced her first litter on the day of the incredible moon-landing.

If you have kept a journal throughout part of your life, you are fortunate because it will undoubtedly help trigger off memories. You can even include sections of this, if you wish, or use them as the nucleus for your book.

Take Yourself Back In Time

When we are young, often seemingly small happenings make a deep and lasting impression upon us, like discovering there is no Father Christmas, for instance. One of my students wrote about his devastating disappointment at being given the wrong kind of bicycle for his twelfth birthday, something he didn't confess to his well-meaning parents until twenty years later. Another related how, at the age of nine, she learned from a spiteful neighbour that the woman she'd always called 'mother' was not her real mother at all.

One class member began producing the most evocative pieces of autobiographical writing I had ever heard. Congratulating her on her wonderful ability to do so, she admitted to having undergone two years of psychotherapy, some years before, during which she had been encouraged to go back in memory to childhood. This, she felt sure, was why she could recall things so vividly.

I, myself, well remember going out into the streets of my small town after a particularly heavy bombing raid, during the last war, and finding the pavements littered with shrapnel and broken glass and hearing that one of my closest friends had been killed. Just recalling that day brings other wartime memories flooding back – waving to GIs as their enormous tanks lumbered past our houses, singing Judy Garland's song from *The Wizard of Oz*, 'Over the Rainbow', in the school shelter during a daytime air-raid; being evacuated to the countryside along with so many others.

One clear recollection of a certain period in your life becomes an 'Open Sesame' to others which will be received with delight and astonishment by your children and grandchildren. After all, it is a part of their history, too. And the more you allow yourself to delve back into the past, the more half-forgotten memories will be awakened.

But, if you are to spend valuable time committing these tales to paper, you need to know who your audience, your reader-ship, will be. If you are aiming at a wider one than the intimate circle of family and perhaps friends, you will need to exaggerate, highlight and embroider the truth a little in order to make your account the more entertaining. The characters portrayed will need to be drawn that little bit larger than life. The drama or humour of situations will have to be heightened and, where necessary, in the interests of telling a good story, painted in rather more glowing colours than perhaps were strictly true.

Those autobiographies which have become best-sellers (leaving aside those by the already famous) have certain qualities in common. They tell of lives that are (or were at a particular period) different from those lived by most of us. They tell of people who had to struggle against difficulties and great odds or who, perhaps, took risks bigger than most in order to achieve a dream or which completely changed their life-style. But, above all, they were told vividly and with humour and compassion.

10

Being Objective

Nancy Hale, in *The Realities of Fiction*, suggests that to interest the reading public in one's life story involves achieving an objectivity which enables you to select from the intriguing scenes that crowd it and to think 'coldly and cunningly about what, in his life, will interest anyone else' and also how that interest can be intensified. She maintains that readers get a satisfaction from autobiographical stories because of the sense of problems shared – that we are all in the same boat in life, adding that '. . . it is as impossible to put down only factual truth into autobiography as it is impossible to keep it out of fiction. One cannot write down one's memories as they really happened. A: one's memory is not that accurate; and B: the attempt is the surest avenue to achieving a weak effect.'

Some of you will be looking as far back as your memory allows, which will probably be to about three years old. Others, though, may have chosen only one particular segment of their lives. Kathy, for instance (who described herself as 'only a housewife'), decided she would like to put on paper a light-hearted account of how she and her husband achieved a lifetime's ambition when, on his retirement, they bought a boat. Never having attempted anything of this kind before, she joined my creative writing class and, week after week, regaled us with hilarious accounts of how they set about first buying their boat, then getting it on to water and, eventually, sailing it around the British Isles and even further. She told her story with a natural humour and ability to see the funny side of things.

Sadly, after a couple of years of trying to fit her writing into a growing number of other leisure activities (including sailing), Kathy stopped coming to class and we missed that bright spot of the week. Did she ever finish her book, I wonder? It was doubly sad because I believed it was potentially worthy of publication. One only has to look at how popular autobiographies of the James Herriot 'vet' variety are to know there is a market ready and waiting for anyone able to produce another in that vein.

Motivation

To get any book published takes a deal of hard work and involves sticking at it when maybe you'd rather be doing something else, like going for a walk or gardening or reading someone else's book. The key word is Choice – and only you can make it. But unless you are strongly motivated with a desire to see your work in print and with the necessary determination to succeed, it is unlikely you will do so.

In times of frighteningly rapid change, such as we've been passing through over the last few decades, when space travel no longer has the power to excite, when travel by plane and car are the 'norm' and killer diseases like tuberculosis and diphtheria are prevented by immunisation, going back to the past can offer some kind of security. There is something somehow *safe* about nostalgia because our memories are sufficiently selective to retain mostly the nice bits, which is probably why it never goes out of fashion. I believe this is largely the reason why collecting antiques is so popular, why so many of us like to haunt junk shops and antique markets, surrounding ourselves with relics of a bygone age.

But, however you decide to relate your story and for whatever purpose, you will have begun to compile a valuable record of what life was like maybe forty, fifty or even more years ago.

If you are one of those who secretly hanker to write a novel (and I'm sure you've heard the saying that everyone has one book in them), then it could be that starting on your life story will spark off an idea for an autobiographical novel, too. But, whatever your aim – complete life story, short separate pieces of autobiography or a novel – the first step is to take yourself back to the past, to the start of it all, and rekindle your earliest memories.

Exercise Find a quiet spot where you will be uninterrupted for a while and try to recall your very first memory, then write a brief account of it. Mention why you think you have retained it and what its significance is. Include as many details as you can, however small. Later on, as your memory becomes reawakened, you will probably find that one thing leads to another and incidents, events and their accompanying details will come flooding back. When they do, write them down, immediately, before they disappear again.

SECTION ONE

Now you're ready to begin

GETTING STARTED

As every writer knows, actually getting started is often the hardest part of the whole operation and, if this is the first time you've tried your hand at the writing game, you're probably feeling even more daunted at the idea of putting all those words on paper. So, now we've discussed the reasons *why* you should do so, let's take a look at *how* to begin.

1. If at all possible, find some space for yourself, even if it is only a table in a corner of a room, where you can not only write but can keep your MS safely in a folder, lay out your notes, photographs or any memorabilia that will help you in your task.

2. Try to organise your daily routine so that you have at least an hour or so *at the same time each day* because our minds are rather like clocks, they work best if wound up regularly.

3. Make a habit of jotting down any ideas, incidents or episodes *immediately* they occur to you. Just a few key words or phrases will be sufficient to ensure you don't forget them because they have a nasty habit of disappearing from your mind, later, leaving you fuming with frustration. Every writer knows the anguish of

having had a marvellous idea for a story, a superb opening for a novel, or a brilliant line of dialogue, at some inconvenient moment, only to find it's completely gone when they try to recapture it. Even if it comes to you in the middle of the night, switch on the light and scribble down a note or two to remind you in the morning. Thus, a wise maxim is: *Always carry a pen and notepad with you.*

4. Sift through desks and drawers for half-forgotten memorabilia which can be an enormous help, at this point. A faded, pressed rose might be a bit of a cliché but, none the less, if you have one stuck inside an old book it must have some significance for you or you wouldn't have put it there, many moons ago. Perhaps you have a piece of yellowing lace that once belonged to your grandmother, or some old, sepia postcards sent from the seaside earlier this century.

   I've always regretted letting an aunt, whilst sorting out a bureau maybe forty years ago, throw away some postcards sent by her brother-in-law from the front in France during the First World War. I remember his poignant comment that the girls over there were not as pretty as in their village. What a treasure trove I might have found, now, had those boxes still been in existence.

   And if, by any stroke of good fortune, you come across old diaries or letters from your parents or grandparents, you have a storehouse of jewels with which to add richness to your book.

5. Collect together any material of this sort and keep it in a box close to hand. Then if, one day, you find you're lacking in inspiration, dipping into it might be enough to start the memories flooding back.

6. Start a simple filing system, using large envelopes (used ones will suit, admirably) in which you can put odds and ends of relevant information until required.

7. Next, brainstorm for ideas of what to include. At this stage, make a note of anything and everything you can think of that might be suitable. You can select and

discard later on, but, for the moment, you are merely collecting together possible material. Again, all you need, now, are key words or phrases to act as memory-joggers. For instance, as I'm planning part of my own life story, I have dozens of headings such as: problem with water supply; buying Beauty; buying and selling Tommy; visiting Frank B., the blacksmith; Charlie P. teaches me to milk and gives us Mathilda, our first hen. Obviously, I can't write them all up at once but those few words are enough to conjure up pictures in my mind and set off the necessary train of thought to get me started.

8. If you have decided to begin with your childhood and your earliest memories, you will need to reawaken the child within you in order to successfully portray that period, which may not be easy. Then, we saw things so much more clearly, everything was larger and brighter than when we became adults. Here, thinking back to the games you enjoyed, perhaps in the school playground (remember the ubiquitous skipping-rope, the game we called Mr Wolf and those gaily-coloured hula hoops?), should release a floodtide of half-forgotten memories. Do you remember the teachers who were probably only in their thirties but who seemed as old as time to you, then? Again, old photographs or long-treasured toys will prove valuable triggers for this section of your story.

9. Bear in mind the maxim that 'people are interested in people' and so think of some of the more colourful people you've known throughout your life and make a note to include some of them. Remember Aunt Beth's seventieth birthday party when Uncle Jake got stoned, or Cousin Jane's wedding and the best man couldn't find the ring? Your family will be highly entertained to hear of such incidents, even though they might not have seemed so amusing at the time.

10. Finally, the main thing is not to frighten yourself by thinking you have to write so many thousand words to make a book. Think of it merely as consisting of a

number of short, separate pieces, as already suggested and which is discussed in greater detail in Section 3 which deals with Article Writing. That way, getting started won't seem such a great hurdle to get over.

Many writers confess that they have great difficulty in making themselves get down to the physical act of writing, itself. They will happily think about it, read books about the subject and even talk about what they intend to write – but actually doing it is a different matter. Many eminent writers devised various gimmicks to help them over this very real psychological barrier. John Steinbeck, for instance, started his working day with a letter to his agent and friend. He would begin by relating quite often trivial things that had occurred the previous day, then ease himself into the novel he was currently engaged upon by discussing what he thought his characters might do or what incidents might occur in the next section.

If skilled and experienced writers find it hard, how much more so will those to whom it is completely new territory? Therefore, just as no one in their right mind would set off on a marathon walk or mountain climb without getting into practice, first, you might find a few 'limbering up' exercises helpful in getting over that initial hurdle of putting pen to paper and beginning your life story.

One of my students, finding it difficult to get on with her novel in isolation and with a young family which left her little spare time for writing, found she made slow but steady progress by producing a short piece for our weekly class. Whatever topic was set for 'homework', she cleverly managed to tailor it to fit a part of her story which was very much based on her own life. The fact that it wasn't in sequence didn't matter – what mattered was that, by doing what were virtually exercises, she was producing fragments of work, rather like making a patchwork quilt, which would eventually become part of her book.

If you would like to 'test the water', first of all, you might like to try this exercise.

Exercise Start as if you were writing a letter to someone you haven't seen for a long time, telling them about something that happened to you. Begin, 'Dear X', then go on to describe the incident without worrying, at this stage, about grammar or style.

The following are a few trigger-topics which, in the past, have resulted in some excellent autobiographical writing by students, any one of which you might find gives you inspiration. Choose one and let it act as a springboard for your returning memories:

- The day they came to . . .
- The move
- The return
- Homesickness
- I never thought I could . . .

Alternatively, you could write it up as if intended for your private journal. As this will be for your own eyes only, you can really let yourself go, putting down anything and everything, your thoughts, feelings and observations. Once you've got the flow going, you should find you can continue until it's time to finish that particular session.

PLANNING YOUR BOOK

Once you've decided on the period your book is to cover, you need to plan the sequence it will follow. Unless you do this, the chances are it will end up a confusing jumble of memories which your reader will not be able to slot into any kind of time-scale. Without working out some kind of plan, there is also the very real danger of trying to cram too much into one short piece of narrative instead of allowing enough space for each important topic.

The main methods of structuring your book are:

Straightforward chronological narrative of events

This might well begin with your birth or earliest memory and finish with the present day or at whatever point you decide upon. Of course, there will be periods when nothing of great importance happened and you can skip over several years quite easily by saying something like:

'The years between eight and thirteen remain hazy in my memory so I can only assume nothing much happened during them. But my fourteenth birthday became a landmark in my life because that was the day . . .'

Or you may prefer to begin by introducing your parents or even your grandparents, thus setting the scene of your own life. Roald Dahl began his *Boy – Tales of Childhood* in this way.

If you choose this plan, you needn't actually write the book in choronological order. If certain episodes come quickly and vividly to mind, it is probably better to get them down on paper, first, while you remember them clearly. In any case, writing up one section will invariably set in motion another and another in a kind of chain reaction as more memories are awakened. Each can then be slotted in place when you begin to bring it all together.

Separate headings

You might have Early Childhood; Schooldays; Growing Up; Family; Grandparents; Holidays; Illness; Romance; Marriage; the War; and so on.

With this method, you can easily collect together your

material, adding to each section as you go along if you think of any other anecdotes or episodes that belong in it. Daphne Rae used this technique in her autobiography, *A World Apart*, a useful one to study if this approach appeals to you.

Another is Paul Bailey's simply but beautifully written *An Immaculate Mistake* in which each short chapter or section carries intriguing titles such as In Error; Confetti; Nicholas Nickleby; Paris 1951; Other People's Relics, and so on.

I suspect this method is what Agatha Christie was describing in *An Autobiography* when she referred to '. . . plunging my hand into a lucky dip and coming up with a handful of assorted memories'. Here, too, you can write each piece in any order you choose.

A single interesting or entertaining period of your life

Many of those autobiographies which have become best-sellers fall into this category. Usually written with the definite aim of publication, they tend to span a few years only and relate humorous, poignant or fascinating accounts of events during that time. If successful, there is likely to be at least one sequel. For instance, Derek Tangye's books describe life out of the 'rat race' growing flowers in Cornwall and with a variety of animals and wildlife. Lilian Beckwith wrote about a period of her life spent in the Hebrides, while Hilda Hollingsworth related her experiences as an evacuee during the Second World War. Here, you have your structure ready-made in terms of years covered.

Starting at a high point in your life

This might be an important turning point or perhaps a dramatic event. For example, did you have a serious illness or accident that changed your life for ever? Did you, perhaps, make a momentous decision that set you on an entirely unexpected course? Do you have an exceptionally dramatic or unusual incident to relate, perhaps the main reason for writing your autobiography? This might be the best way to 'hook' your reader before going back to the beginning of your life.

Choosing the right starting-point will help you plan the rest of your story more easily. Let me illustrate this by describing how Jean Waddell (see *Incident in Iran* in Section 6) planned the structure of her autobiography, beginning with a truly dramatic incident.

A deeply spiritual person, Jean had already had a brush with death as a child and believed that God had saved her on this last occasion for a specific purpose. She was also able to see a definite thread running through her life and so, having decided to begin her story at a high point of drama when she was shot and left for dead while living and working in Iran she then went back to her childhood on the east coast of Scotland. This is where, she believes, it all began for her during what she remembers as lively church services, sitting between two favourite maiden aunts and, as a rather extrovert tot, singing along with the Salvation Army band on the sandy beaches of her home town, every summer.

She mapped out the rest of her life story in chronological order under various headings: growing up beside the sea; illness; schooldays; first job; the war; and so on. The end of her book will be a return to the beginning, telling of what happened in the months after she recovered from the shooting in hospital and of her life following that to the present day with her faith as strong as ever.

Dividing Up Your Book

You need to consider, also, how you intend breaking up your book into easily digestible chunks. The most obvious way is to divide it into chapters, in which case, shortish ones are usually best. If you aim for between 1500 and 2000 words at most, it will help make your book easier to pick up and put

21

down, at odd moments (say, at bedtime when many people like to read for a short while before going to sleep). So let's take a look at the way in which these should be structured.

Each needs to begin with a 'hook' to encourage the reader to continue the story and giving a clue as to what it will be about. If you spend some time analysing published autobiographies (which will be time well spent), you will see that each chapter revolves around one particular incident or event. Although the book, as a whole, will progress logically from start to finish, none the less, unlike a novel which has a strong narrative thread or storyline running through it, building up to a climax, an autobiography is episodic in style and content so that each chapter stands virtually alone.

We will deal with beginnings and endings in more detail, later, but, in planning your chapters, remember to finish each at a point which will create in the reader a tiny glow of contentment, a willingness to close the book until the next time he settles himself down with it and can take up your story, once more.

To illustrate structure, let's take a look at one or two successful autobiographies. The first chapter of Derek Tangye's *Somewhere a Cat is Waiting*, for instance, deals with the cat, Monty's, first appearance and lets us know the author is not a cat lover, only, three months earlier, he had married someone who was. Chapter Two centres around his partial acceptance of its presence but only as a kitchen cat, while the next shows him beginning to play with Monty. Subsequent chapters follow various exploits involving the cat – how he responded to bird-life, including an owl; how he was in danger from a maurauding fox, and so forth.

The first chapter of Louise Brindley's *They Must Have Seen Me Coming* centres on her going for a job at a residential old people's home. The next is about her first days working there.

Writing A Synopsis

You may find it helpful to prepare a brief synopsis or outline of the way you see your book developing. It doesn't have to be very long or detailed and, like most novelists, who usually write one before they start work on the book itself, you don't have to stick to it if, as you go along, you find a better route for your journey. Keep it simple and let it serve merely as a quick reminder of where you're going.

It might run something like this: First memory – seeing my new brother in my mother's arms. Schooldays – primary and horror of boarding-school. Visiting grandparents and meeting Uncle George for first time. Arguing with father, refusing to enter family firm, enlisting in army and not returning home for five years.

Continue on the same lines, covering whatever period you intend to include in your book because time spent on planning the sequence and the method you feel happiest with will undoubtedly make the actual writing that much easier for you.

ORGANISING AND SELECTING YOUR MATERIAL

The biggest problem you're likely to find is that you have too much material, so sorting it out, putting it into some kind of order and selecting what to use and what to leave out, will undoubtedly save you many hours of unnecessary work. Remember that with any form of writing we are practising an art form and, as Henry James said: 'Life is all inclusion and confusion. Art is all discrimination and selection.'

A while ago, I was asked to take a critical look at an autobiography which spanned the author's life from age two to sixteen. The author had had an exceptionally interesting childhood and it all made gripping reading but she hadn't been selective enough in the abundance of material she had

23

to choose from. The typescript ran to more than 800 pages (nearly 200,000 words). Clearly, it was far too long to even be considered by a publisher and needed to be drastically cut. The task of reducing it by half was willingly and enthusiastically undertaken but, even then, it was still too long for one volume and needed to be two separate ones.

Thus, once you have brainstormed for ideas of what to include, mapped out a plan or structure for your book, you need to organise your material before starting the selection process. The following is a simple method:

1. Clear a large working surface, preferably one where you can leave everything undisturbed for a few hours, at least.

2. Write out on pieces of paper or thin cardboard all the ideas, incidents and so on you've thought of, with approximate dates or age, e.g. measles (six); scarlet fever/quarantine (ten); appendicitis/hospital (thirteen); first pet/Joey the budgie (seven); camping holiday (1938); going to visit Great-Aunt Louisa (five-ish); and so on.

3. Sort them roughly into groups, depending on the proposed structure of your book, so that when you start writing you won't miss any out.

4. On a large sheet of paper (the plain side of a roll of wallpaper would fit the purpose admirably) write the period to be covered, then pencil in dates of important incidents and episodes. If you can pin it to a wall and leave it there until you've finished writing, this should be a tremendous help. Then, whenever you think of something else you might want to include (which you are sure to do as you go along), all you need to do is make a note of it. If you can't keep it on view all the time, it is easily rolled up and put away until you want it again.

These are only suggestions to help make your task easier and seem less daunting but you will eventually find the working method best suited to yourself. Now you are ready to start the selection process.

The only criterion you need apply is: will this incident be of sufficient interest to others, whether my family or strangers? The fact that you had measles when you were six is probably totally irrelevant unless your life was in danger or it coincided with some other important event such as a brother or sister being born, or it has awakened in you other memories, perhaps of another family member who affected your life. Of course, you might wish to describe how measles was treated, all those years ago.

What you must now do is sift through everything you've assembled and *select* the key moments of your life, the colourful and/or influential characters who moved through it: in fact, all the things and people who helped form you, make you the person you are, excising anything that was inconsequential. The word to keep in mind is *significant*. If a certain incident had a great effect on you, changed your life in some way, then it should be included. If it made little impression upon you, at the time, then leave it out. Suppose, for instance, a cousin came to stay with you for a whole month when you were eight years old. Unless he taught you how to fish, told so many lies about you that you hated him for ever after or, perhaps, as you learned later, had been sent to stay because his mother was dying, making you feel guilty for the rest of your life that you hadn't been nicer to him, say, there isn't much point in mentioning it.

Bear in mind, too, that some experiences will be common to many – during the last war, for example. One lady showed me part of her autobiography which dealt, in the main, with her years in the ATS. Although it related one exciting (to her) incident when, on their way to Africa, they were dive-bombed by the enemy, it wasn't sufficiently *different* to the experiences of thousands of others during that period. However, when I read a brief history of her childhood, family background and subsequent life, it was obvious she had masses of material simply begging to be written up and all quite individual to herself.

Here, if you haven't already done so, you need to make the decision whether or not to tell your story 'warts and all'. Will you be able, or even want, to include the more painful parts? Are you willing to relate them candidly and truthfully? Sometimes, of course, the fact that some of those once close to us are now dead gives us greater freedom, as Paul Bailey observed about his autobiography, *An Immaculate Mistake*.

Now you're ready to actually start writing – so where to begin? You may find it best to start with one or two short, complete pieces, as already suggested. For the first one, you should choose a dramatic or significant incident in your life (not necessarily in childhood) or maybe describe a colourful character, someone you will never forget. Another idea is to dig down for your earliest memory and write about that.

However, if you decide you want to commence writing your autobiography at the beginning and work through it, chronologically, then the section headed Beginnings is˙ designed to help you with this.

Lastly, what else might you include, if your book is intended for private viewing only? The following items could usefully be added:

- Family sayings
- Poems, either your own or those written by a parent or other close relative
- Family recipes that have been handed down
- Letters or diary extracts
- Newspaper cuttings
- A drawing of your family tree

But, once you start writing, you will find that one memory will trigger off another and another and so on until, before you realise it, you will have written an entire book.

MEMORY JOGGERS

'Writing, like life itself, is a voyage of discovery.'
Henry Miller

Just as when you're undertaking any journey for the first time, it is helpful to have certain signposts to guide you on your way. For the purposes of writing your life story, these can be anything that jogs your memory awake, aiding the recall of events and incidents in colour and detail; any significant points or moments in your life. You can make your own list, adding to it as others occur to you, but below are a few with which you might start.

- Birth
- A turning point or major decision
- First Love/Romance
- Marriage
- Children
- Religion, if it played an important part in your life
- War
- Schooldays/College
- A special place
- First job/career
- Death of someone close
- Retirement
- Illness
- Travel
- Parents
- Grandparents
- Siblings
- People who have influenced you/characters you'll never forget
- Holidays
- Festivities such as Christmas (Hogmanay in Scotland, Thanksgiving in the US, 14 July in France and so on, depending on country and culture)

- Friends
- Absorbing hobbies/pastimes
- Unfulfilled dreams/ambitions
- Favourite games/toys
- Pets.

As you make your list, leave room to add key words or phrases. Then, when you're ready to write up one particular topic in greater detail, take a fresh piece of paper and give it a heading so you can begin to jot down anything at all even vaguely connected with it. You can start the selection process, later, when you come to working on it with the intention of writing one complete section.

With this, you can start at any point at all in your life story. You might like to copy Agatha Christie's 'lucky dip' method, which is similar to one of my students' 'patchwork quilt' way of writing mentioned earlier. It will be easy enough to place these into some kind of order when you start to bring the book together as a whole, later.

Lateral Thinking or 'Mind-Mapping'

You might find it helpful to try this process. It has been proved that the brain absorbs information in a non-linear way rather than the way most of us have been trained to think, that is in linear fashion, making notes in list-form. To use this method, place the subject word or phrase in the centre of the page and run spokes outwards from it as your mind comes up with anything that is remotely connected to it. For example, suppose you chose Retirement from the list of memory joggers, write that in the centre, then add anything to do with that topic as it occurs to you. For instance, you might come up with: fear; loss of identity; leaving present; leaving 'do'; more leisure time; extra hobbies; moving to smaller house; and so on.

A number of books have been written on this subject of 'mind-mapping', including one by Tony Buzan called *Use Your Head*.

Let us, now, take a look at a few of those headings and see what might be included under them.

Birth

Many of you will decide to start your autobiography at the logical point of your birth even though everything you know of that event will have been related to you by others. Start by making a list of everything you have been told, perhaps by your mother, or know from other sources, including your birth-weight, where you were born, time and date, and so on. How did your parents choose your first name(s)? Was there anything special about either of your parents – age, for instance, or nationality? Did your arrival coincide with any world events that might add to its interest? Perhaps you were born on the day the First World War broke out or on Armistice Day.

If I were to start my own life story with my birth, I would probably begin like this.

Looking at me, now, mother of three and grandmother of two, who would guess that I weighed in at birth at a mere five pounds; that I was, according to my mother, a weak, sickly baby whom she never thought would grow to adulthood? Not that I can remember being anything other than fit and healthy (apart from succumbing to the usual childish ailments). What I can remember, with something like a shudder, is being pumped full of 'tonics' – to make me eat, calm me down, increase the iron in my blood. Not to mention the ubiquitous dose of Syrup of Senna, every Friday night without fail, to keep me 'regular'. Pills, nauseous liquids, sticky toffee-like substances – all were forced down my unwilling throat for most of my childhood.

Giving birth, in those days, could not have been a pleasant experience, with no pain-relief available unless you could afford to pay for it. My mother told me, once, how her sister-in-law, having had two children of her own,

29

advised her to pay for a doctor to attend my birth so an anaesthetic could be administered, when necessary. This she did but, none the less, vowed she would have no more children. Hence I grew up an only – and a lonely – child, envious of others belonging to large families and always feeling an outsider. In time, I, too, made a vow: never to have an only child. It was a vow I kept.

Hobbies/Pastimes/Leisure Interests

Those who have an absorbing hobby of any kind are fortunate indeed, especially if it is one which doesn't necessitate being actively fit so that age is no barrier. Unknowingly, we may well have influenced others through these, introducing them to a totally new world that will bring them great pleasure, too.

If I were to write on this subject, I would want to include opera. I would tell how, if I had had a fairy godmother (as in all the best fairytales) to grant me a wish, I would have begged to become an opera singer, a prima donna. Oh, the dreams I dreamed, as a child, of being 'discovered' by an impresario! And that would, quite naturally, have led me to explain *why; why* I loved listening to the great singers of the world.

I was fortunate enough to have three maiden aunts living close to my home, as I was growing up. These aunts (like so many others of their generation, unmarried because the men who should have been their husbands had been slaughtered on the battlefields of the First World War), had set about educating themselves as best they could. They had a book-case filled with novels by all the popular Victorian and Edwardian writers, a veritable treasure-chest for me. They also had one of those now sought-after antique wind-up gramophones, together with a large collection of His Master's Voice recordings of operatic arias sung by the likes of Caruso, Galli-Curci and Dame Nellie Melba. There were also hauntingly sad songs performed by the famous Irish tenor, John McCormack, as well as more by Heddle Nash and others. Thus, unconsciously, my tastes were being formed, as were my dreams, and so my aunts would come, quite naturally, into anything I were to write about pastimes.

Entertainment

You could include, here, entertainments of the past, some of which are experiencing a resurgence of popularity, such as old time music-hall and tea dances.

And do you remember the magic of your first visit to a theatre or to the cinema? I can recall the first time I was taken to the cinema and saw a Charlie Chaplain film. When I was about six years old, my mother and I had been to stay with her sister in the country, leaving my father behind. He came to meet us off the train and took us to the pictures (as we used to call the cinema). I didn't fully understand, then, but the reason for our 'holiday' without him was that he and my mother had quarrelled, violently, and she had been considering leaving him for good. He must have missed us, however, and had written begging us to come back. Thus, seeing that film with both my parents (an unusual treat), has remained vivid in my memory.

The War

Although there have, sadly, been several wars, this century, it was the Second World War which played a tremendous part in the lives of many people, often changing them for ever. I have heard numerous bizarre incidents related by those who went to war. One such, recounted by J., a friend now dead, told of how, after being ill, he had somehow lost his battalion in North Africa and set off to find them. But, because of the uncertainties of finding food, he managed to acquire a hen which travelled with him across miles of desert, providing him with sufficient protein in the form of eggs until he finally caught up with his unit.

For anyone who lived through the blitz, the experience will be seared on their memories forever. Air-raid wardens with tin hats and gas-masks slung over their shoulders, the eerie wail of sirens warning of a coming air-raid and, when it was over, the high-pitched shriek of the All Clear; the camaraderie of the shelters, singing songs, reading by candle-light, the emergency food-boxes; the coming out on to the streets to find them littered with often still-hot shards of twisted metal, pavements crunchy underfoot with shattered windows.

Were you evacuated to the countryside or sent across the Atlantic to America or Canada for safety? Such traumatic experiences often coloured lives ever after. Then there were ration-books, identity cards to be carried everywhere, posters warning that 'Careless Talk Costs Lives', and the traitor broadcaster, William Joyce with his 'Germany Calling', a man who paid for it with his life, in the end.

War on any scale may have changed your entire outlook on life or influenced you in some way. Have you ever been on a Peace March, for instance? Were you, or your father, maybe, a conscientious objector in the last war? What stand did you take over the Gulf War?

An autobiography is one place where you can make known your opinions and beliefs. Although you shouldn't 'stand on a soapbox' and preach or you will quickly lose your audience, if you feel strongly about anything, don't be afraid to include it in your book: it is an essential part of yourself.

Schooldays

Times have changed considerably in the field of education, over the past few decades. When I was growing up, it wasn't easy to go on to any form of higher education unless you came from a comfortably-off or academic family and even if intelligent children from poorer homes won a scholarship, they could not always take up their place at grammar school. At what age did you leave school? Fourteen was the normal leaving age, years ago, but my own mother, being the eldest of a large family, was forced to leave at twelve.

What was your experience in education? Did it dramatically change your life in some way? Do you still feel you missed out for some reason? Do you think that formal education is overrated, perhaps?

A friend of mine carried around within her throughout most of her adult life a bitter resentment that, because of family circumstances, she was unable to go to college and continue her education. Instead she started work at the age of fourteen, delivering milk by horse and cart. Many years later, relating some of her life experiences to a young Canadian woman, she was brought up sharp by the other's response; it was sheer envy. 'Aren't you lucky to have done all that! How I wish I had.' And, suddenly, my friend saw her past in a different light. Certainly, she hadn't had the higher education she had longed for – but she had had a different kind, one we can only acquire through *living*. From that day on, her bitterness (though not all her regrets) left her.

Games/Toys

What games do you remember playing as a child? Many of them are quite different, today, from when most of us were children. Games played in the school playground used to follow a pattern, throughout the year. There would be a period when the top and whip was popular; then there was the yo-yo, made of brightly-coloured wood, which bounced up and down on its string as if by magic. A favourite of the girls was the skipping-rope while both boys and girls played hopscotch and marbles. Recently, I discovered that marbles have made a come-back and I enjoyed a game of 'ollies' (as we used to call them) with my six-year-old grandson, much to his astonishment.

Did you have a favourite toy – a teddy-bear, perhaps, or golden-haired china doll? Recalling that may well bring other memories flooding back.

Illness

The treatment of illnesses has altered dramatically, over the last fifty years. In an earlier generation, tuberculosis was a scourge that often swept through whole families. Diphtheria was a killer and sufferers from scarlet fever and other infectious diseases were quarantined, either in hospital or behind heavy curtains impregnated with disinfectant.

In the early part of this century, too, a dreaded question in many homes would be: Can we afford the doctor? Thus, many families would turn to herbal remedies, in the first instance, or ask the local pharmacist to make something up, only calling in the doctor as a last resort.

Do you remember having your chest rubbed with pungent camphorated oil when you had a bad cold? Or perhaps your mother used goose grease? If your father had lumbago, did he rub his back with embrocation then swathe it in red flannel? Did you ever suffer from chilblains and smother them with that sticky, strong-smelling green ointment? Think back to when you were sick and what treatment you received. Today's young people will probably be intrigued although, interestingly, there seems to have been a renewed and growing interest in 'natural' remedies, over recent years.

First Job/Career

If there is one event in our early life few of us will ever forget, it is surely our first job and, in particular, that first day. One moment, we were in the safe, known environment of school and, the next, catapulted into the strange, frightening wider world where we were supposed to act like adults. Younger members of your family will, I'm sure, love to read about how you felt, then, because it will undoubtedly mirror their own feelings and may help them realise they are not alone in experiencing fear and uncertainty.

How did you choose your career? Did you go into it

because of your parents' influence, perhaps because it was expected that you would follow in your father's footsteps? Did you regret your choice, later, but decide to stick with it or did you change direction after some momentous soul-searching? Today, it is accepted that many women will have careers and return to them after they have had their babies, but it was not quite so easy a generation ago. How was it for you?

Travel/Holidays/Festivities

Did you have an annual seaside holiday when you were a child? Did you go camping or stay in one of those ubiquitous guesthouses run by that forgotten breed of landlady? How did you celebrate Christmas or your own particular national festivity? Travel by air, today, is the norm but not so long ago it was looked upon as a great adventure. When did you first board a plane and do you remember how you felt? In Section 6, you will read a delightful account of an annual holiday taken in Scotland, at the beginning of this century.

Entertainment/Music/Songs

Songs are great activators for conjuring up a particular period. Songs such as 'Tipperary' and 'Pack Up Your Troubles' re-create, instantly, the First World War, even for those too young to remember anything of its horrors. Old music-hall lyrics, too, have a nostalgic charm of their own, recalling the Edwardian era and popularity of performers like George Robey and others. Then, the Second World War brought us such songs as 'Run Rabbit, Run', 'The White Cliffs of Dover' sung, of course, by Vera Lynn, nicknamed the Forces' Sweetheart, and many others.

One great advantage of making a list of 'memory joggers' is that you never know where they will lead you. Thus, it becomes an exciting journey of discovery as fresh ideas, snippets of half-forgotten memories occur to you.

Exercise Close your eyes and picture an object that was significant in some way to you, either in childhood or later. Describe it, relating the particular circumstances associated with it. You will probably find previously long-forgotten emotions coming to the surface connected with whatever it was.

BEGINNINGS

The beginning of any piece of writing is of paramount importance because, if that isn't sufficiently interesting, no one is likely to read any further. The first sentence, paragraph, or page of a book, is the bait on the hook which will either catch your readers or lose them, perhaps forever. Thus, it is time well spent in getting your opening right.

Your beginning needs to intrigue in some way, persuading readers that they simply must know what happens next and, therefore, must carry on reading. There are various 'tricks' to ensure this. For instance, you could make a statement that will startle or shock the reader. Or open with a line of dialogue – always a useful ploy with any kind of writing. Or perhaps with a colourful description of a place or a person. But, almost immediately, you need to give certain information: who, where, what and when. The other two of Kipling's 'six honest serving men' (referred to later in this section) are how and why, which should be introduced in due course.

We will look at writing up short, complete sections of autobiography as articles in Section 3: here I want to concentrate on your book as a whole. With this, you may only have the first page in which to attract and keep your reader's attention (and the editor's, initially, if it is intended for publication) to have any chance of success, so studying the openings of published autobiographies will pay dividends when you start working on your own.

I have chosen several by authors who are not household names (as well as one by an established writer and one who is now well-known as a result of her autobiography), which all have something in common: page-turning quality. We are *compelled* to read on to find out 'what happens next' – which is what story-telling is all about.

The opening of any piece of writing, long or short, must set the 'tone' for the rest of it. If it is to be light-hearted and humorous, we need to know that immediately. If it is to be wryly amusing yet also moving, again, the opening page should tell us that. If it is pure nostalgia for more leisurely times long since past, or has a serious thread running through it, similarly, the reader should be given a hint of this at the beginning. So now let's take a look at some autobiographies that have achieved publication.

Not Quite Heaven by Brenda Courtie

Funny things, my knees. Sort of fair weather friends. Most of the time they're on my side, supporting me when I stand or walk, or pumping like pistons to propel me on my bike, or getting me down to pray or scrub with never a hint of a twinge.

But comes the time when I get up in front of an audience and the knees go on strike. They quiver with fear and mutter: 'Oh no! Count us out. You're on your own for this one!'

Brenda Courtie is a vicar's wife and we are given a clue to the importance of the Church in her life by the words 'getting me down to pray'. By suggesting that her knees have a life independent of their owner and allowing them to speak, the author immediately establishes the book's humorous tone. And, even though we suspect it may also contain some kind of 'message', we can be certain it will not be laboured. Indeed, if it were, she would quickly lose her audience.

A Child in the Forest by Winifred Foley

At home, I was 'our Poll' to my little sister and brother; 'my little wench' to Dad; 'a regular little 'oman' sometimes, but often 'a slomucky little hussy' to my sorely tried Mam; to the ribald boys, 'Polish it behind the door', and to my best friend Gladys just 'Poll'. Gladys was an only child, always clean and tidy, but she never turned up her nose at playing with me, even when the school nurse found lice in my hair, and my neck was covered in flea bites.

By introducing us to her family and her 'best friend' through the device of divulging the nicknames each gave to her, the author quickly suggests something of her childhood background. And, from that last sentence, it is clear her story is going to be told 'warts and all'. I think it is obvious why it had such wide appeal, telling, as it did, of a time that has gone forever and full of real and colourful characters.

A Hovel In The Hills by Elizabeth West

'Your *what*?' said Alan. 'My brassiere straps,' I repeated. 'They're caught up in the mangle again.'

With the air of a man born to shoulder many burdens, he accompanied me to the mangle house. Why-don't-you-get-yourself-liberated-and-save-us-both-a-lot-of-trouble was the general drift of his comments as he eased the twisted straps from the snarl-up around the oily cogs.

Later, whilst hopefully dabbing at grease-caked broderie anglaise, I reflected upon the problems of washday in the wilderness. And it occurred to me that I am possibly the only woman in Britain whose washing is liable to end up dirtier than it started.

The effectiveness of opening with dialogue is demonstrated, here. Instantly, we are dragged into the story about to unfold, almost whether we want to be or not. We learn quite a lot about the author, her long-suffering husband and their situation by deft references to 'the mangle house' and 'washday in the wilderness'. There can be little doubt that this is to be a humorous account of a 'back to nature' type of living. A less skilful writer might have begun in a much duller way with, perhaps, something on the lines of: 'We had just gone to live in an isolated cottage in Wales and this was my first washday.'

A World Apart by Daphne Rae

I was born on August 15, 1933, in the Gaulle Face Nursing Home, Colombo, Ceylon, which has now been renamed Sri Lanka. My address was more romantic than my birth. I have since been told that my entry into society was long and painful. The screams from the labour ward were horrific and the doctor had his shirt torn by the frightened and angry patient. At last the child was born. After months of discomfort and the indignity of labour, a well-formed nine-pounder greeted the mother face to face. It was the final insult for I turned out to be a girl.

Although this book opens with a plain statement of fact, where and when the author was born, the place was different and exotic. The following sentences describe, unusually, the actual birth while the final paragraph strikes a poignant note, hinting at the future, somewhat imperfect, relationship of mother and daughter.

They Must Have Seen Me Coming by Louise Brindley

Snow as fluffy and delicate as white mimosa slapped me gently in the face. A seagull cut through the grey November sky. The smell of seaweed tickled my nostrils. I had arrived at Eastmarch on Sea.

'Taxi, Miss?' I blinked at the man through a flurry of flakes.

'That depends,' I said, 'on how far it is to Brown's Employment Agency in Liddle Street.'

He jerked his head in the direction of the main street. 'First turning on the left.'

Brief descriptions, using the senses of sight, touch and smell, skilfully set the scene, here: a good example of 'brush-strokes' in operation. Different in style to the other openings but, fairly obviously, the story will be light-hearted in tone.

An Immaculate Mistake by Paul Bailey

'You were our mistake,' said my mother. 'You ought not to be here, by rights.'

She was old now, and letting go of her secrets. This one, she knew, would be of particular interest to me.

'We didn't plan to have you, is what I'm saying. People like us had to be very careful when it came to having children. You took me by surprise, and your poor father, too. That was typical of you – determined to be different even before you were born.'

A wry note is struck, immediately, with this opening, calculated to make us curious about both the author and his mother. Again, starting with a line of dialogue makes it almost impossible for us not to read on.

Beyond the Nursery Window by Ruth Plant

It was opening the old box that did it. First, it was the scent of things which is a marvellous activator of memory. That indefinable mixture of smells which resembles no known mixture in the list of famous perfumiers, but which has a subtlety of its own.

I was back in the world of childhood, in the security of the nursery with Nanny sitting by the shaded oil-lamp working at a new smock for me, and my brother in his dressing-gown chuckling over some recent joke in the *Boy's Own Paper*.

This plunges us into times long past with its flavour of pure nostalgia. That first, short sentence subtly suggests letting a genie out of a magic bottle. Phrases like 'by the shaded oil-lamp' and '*Boys Own Paper*' immediately set the scene and establish the period without recourse to long descriptions. And the title, itself, followed by the reference to 'Nanny', clues us into the authors home background.

Each of these beginnings promises something more, further fascinating revelations about the author's life, about the people involved in it, if only you will read on. Note how each, in its own way, seems to be talking directly to you, telling you how it was. Many years ago, at the start of her writing career, Monica Dickens received the following advice from her publisher. He told her to imagine herself entering a room, attracting everyone's attention by saying, 'Hey, listen to what happened to me,' then telling them. Good advice for anyone writing their life story.

Exercise Close your eyes and take yourself back to childhood. Picture a scene in your mind as vividly as you can, then write an opening paragraph to either your book or a particular chapter.

ENDINGS

I hope we're all agreed that a good beginning is of paramount importance or we will quickly lose our potential reader. Then, once having captured his or her attention, we need to keep it by making full use of those fictional techniques we shall be looking at in the next section. Finally, if our book is to be put down with a feeling of contentment, we have to make sure it *ends* on the right note and in the right place.

Choosing that place is perhaps partly instinctive – but that is not of much help when this is the first time you've tried to write something of this nature. So I will try to offer some guidelines for both chapter-endings and the book as a whole.

- Each chapter-ending should be aesthetically pleasing, that is it should leave readers feeling satisfied that that particular segment of your story has reached a natural conclusion. They can then put it down until they are ready to pick it up, again, later. This method is especially

41

suitable if you've used the separate-headings approach so that each chapter is complete in itself.

- If you've used a chronological structure, then try to end each chapter on a subtle note of suspense so that the reader can't bear to leave it and simply has to carry on to the next chapter to find out what happened next.

- So far as your book as a whole is concerned, you can end it at any point in your life you choose – so long as you make it *satisfying* as well as appropriate in some way. If you've brought it right up to the present moment, you might have something simple on the lines of:

I'm now approaching my ... birthday and I've seen changes that would have been unbelievable to my parents. I wonder what the next twenty years will bring and how I'll describe *them?* You'll have to wait and find out – and so will I.

Not only would an ending like this aptly sum up the author as being a lively optimist; wouldn't it, with its rather defiant 'cocking a snook' at life, make you hope there would be a next instalment?

Examples of chapter endings

Twopence to Cross the Mersey by Helen Forrester
Chapter Two ends: 'Somehow we all squeezed into the taxi, a hungry, forlorn group too tired to talk.'
This finishes at a definite point – getting into the taxi. But that final sentence makes us eager to know what happens next to that sad little family.

Hovel in the Hills by Elizabeth West

Having bought and moved into their cottage in Wales, the new owners set about renovating, reading up everything they could about the subject but without finding much that was of use to them.

Chapter Two ends: 'Hafod, it seemed, wasn't the sort of cottage that people wrote books about.'
A neat, satisfactory point at which to end a chapter, hinting that there is much more to learn about the cottage, if we read

on, even though it isn't a suitable subject for a book – which, of course, is exactly what it is!

Examples of book endings

The way the *book* finishes, too, must leave the reader metaphorically, at least, breathing a contented sigh as he puts it down for the last time. If it covers only a portion of the author's life, he should hope for a sequel to it.

An Immaculate Mistake by Paul Bailey

'I wept, then, for both my parents. He had cursed Esther from his deathbed, while my mother held him in her restraining hands. The memory of that name on his lips must have come to her often in her long, devoted widowhood.'

Because he said the book was partly to celebrate something of the ordinariness of his parents' lives, this seems to strike an appropriate note. To me, it 'feels' right. After relating various episodes and incidents from childhood to adulthood, starting with his mother telling him: 'You were our mistake,' he finally weeps for his dead parents. That part of his life is now behind him and, presumably, he can go forward, having put to rest some of his ghosts.

Twopence to Cross the Mersey by Helen Forrester

'Hot in the palm of my hand was a half-crown, the most important coin I was ever to possess. I was to spend seven years in evening schools and I managed in each subsequent year to win a small scholarship . . . I bared my yellow teeth in a smile of pure happiness, charged across the threshold and galloped up the [school] stairs.'

This clearly heralds the end of one period of her life but leaves it open for a sequel which, in fact, she did go on to write.

Hovel in the Hills ends with the author telling us that Hafod was a good place to come home to, leaving the reader feeling warm and comfortable and *satisfied*.

I hope these few examples of chapter and book endings give you some ideas of how to end your own.

FINDING YOUR VOICE

'Words are all we have.'

Samuel Beckett

Chekhov once said that the essence of good style is simplicity. The best piece of advice, therefore, is to keep your writing simple. That isn't to say you should invariably use short sentences, short words and never introduce colourful imagery. On the contrary, if you are to make your life story a 'good read', you should aim for variety – variety of texture and structure.

1. Juxtapose a longish sentence (not *too* long, though) with a couple of short ones, and the same with paragraphs.
2. Find new ways of describing things, avoiding clichés or stale, hackneyed phrases. Don't tell us your mother's eyes were bright as stars (that's been said countless times before), tell us, instead, they were like ox-eye daisies after a spring shower. Look at how other writers describe people, not to copy them but to give you ideas as to how you might bring to life those in your book. One of my all-time favourite pieces of imagery is by Dylan Thomas in *Daydreams and Nightmares*: 'The over-filled bowl of his pipe smouldered among his whiskers like a little burning hayrick on a stick.' Doesn't that create a wonderful picture and don't you just wish you could have thought of it, yourself? I know I do.

   The use of fresh, original similes and metaphors will, without doubt, greatly enhance your writing.
3. Be specific. If you don't know, find out and if you can't find out, it's probably best to leave it out. In other words, be sure of your facts before you refer to an event because, if you've got it wrong, you can be sure someone will spot it. But don't forget that wonderful tool – your imagination. If you can't actually remember what the weather was like on the day of the incident you are relating, so long as it is unlikely to be memorable to

44

others, in any way, *imagine* it to help create a complete picture in the reader's mind. Say: 'A hot sun beat down from a cloudless blue sky on the day I first met my brother', or, 'Rain fell from lowering clouds the day my sister was born', rather than, 'I don't remember what the weather was like on the day . . .' In this way, too, symbolism plays a part in evoking atmosphere because the fact that it was a sunny day suggests to the reader that the ensuing relationship with your brother was a good one or that it wasn't with your sister.

4. Remember that most of us like facts (why else should quiz programmes be so popular?) so provide them, where appropriate. Think of Rudyard Kipling's useful advice:

> I keep six honest serving men
> (They taught me all I knew);
> Their names are WHAT and WHY and WHEN
> And HOW and WHERE and WHO.

This is where taking the trouble to undertake a little research can make all the difference to the level of interest in a particular section. A student of mine came across a book which was a goldmine of dates of events, large and small, during this century. It proved a tremendous aid to her memory when it came to fitting incidents from her own life into the wider context of British history.

5. While it goes without saying that your grammar should be correct, your writing should never be so formal that it becomes stilted. A wise maxim is to write in the way you speak. Forget those strictures by your English teacher at school that you should never start a sentence with and or but, for instance. Nowadays, this is not only acceptable but often preferable as a means of adding emphasis. It can make for tighter prose, as you will realise if you study modern fiction and journalism. For example: 'It wasn't until I became an adult that I realised why. And then it was too late to change things.' By breaking that up into two

sentences, starting the second one with 'And', the focus is sharpened.

In other words, write for the ear, not the eye. *Hear* the words as you put them down, either in your head or actually saying them out loud, listening to the rhythm of your sentences to make sure they *sound* right. And this includes using contractions (I won't; you can't, and so on) in narrative as well as conversation. Remember the words of Hazlitt, the celebrated essayist: 'No style is good that is not fit to be spoken or read aloud with effect.'

6. Using powerful verbs rather than relying on adverbs makes for more effective prose. For example, writing: 'My grandfather strode everywhere' is better than: 'My grandfather walked everywhere quickly'. Too many adverbs tend to weaken a piece of writing.

7. Similarly, be chary of too many adjectives. 'If the noun is good and the verb is strong, you almost never need an adjective,' said writer J. Anthony Lukas. And Mark Twain remarked in humorous vein: 'When you catch an adjective, kill it.' Then, more seriously, 'As to the adjective: when in doubt, strike it out.'

8. It is generally considered better to use the active voice rather than the passive because it makes for stronger writing, being more positive. For example: 'My grandmother baked the most delicious apple pie I've ever tasted', rather than: 'The apple pies baked by my grandmother were the most delicious I've ever tasted'.

9. The simple past tense (I said; he persisted; she went) is normally used in narrative and is certainly the easiest to handle. However, the present tense, if used judiciously, can often create a greater sense of immediacy. So, if you wanted to experiment, you might like to try writing specific sections or chapters this way. For example: 'I am six years old and visiting my Grandmother Thomson for the first time. She is very old and her skin is like a wrinkly apple.'

10. Back to simplicity of style. Don't try to be too literary', using words and phrases which don't come naturally to

you but which you think will sound good, or you risk ending up with pretentious-sounding 'purple passages' that intrude into the story you are telling.

11. An autobiography is normally narrated in the first person, the 'I' form, for the obvious reason that, as defined by my dictionary, it is a memoir of one's life, written by oneself. Told in the third person (Mary said, Harry thought), it would be secondhand and so not, strictly speaking, an autobiography. It would also be in danger of losing its *immediacy*, that valuable ingredient that drags the reader into a story by making them feel *they are there with you* vicariously living your experiences. Flora Thompson's *Lark Rise to Candleford* is the only example I can call to mind where the story is related in the third person through the eyes of the child, Laura. But it would be wise not to try to emulate this for the reasons mentioned and also to avoid possible problems with keeping to a single viewpoint.

    However, try to keep the 'I' as unobtrusive as is compatible with the fact that you are relating your personal life history. This is not so difficult as it might appear and, at the revision stage, you will see places where it could easily be omitted without affecting the meaning.

12. Lastly, if you want to try something different, you might like to experiment with writing in the form of letters or a diary. This method could prove especially useful if you are feeling slightly inhibited about setting down your story on paper. If you were to think of it as a series of letters to your son or daughter, for instance, or merely recording it in a diary for yourself, it might enable you to write in a natural, flowing style that would avoid any of the pitfalls mentioned here.

The fact that you are producing your autobiography solely for the eyes of your own intimate circle shouldn't mean not bothering about *how* it is written. If it is to remain a testament to your existence, perhaps to be handed down to generation after generation, you will want to feel you've written it in the best way you can. And taking care over style, finding your own particular 'voice', will help ensure it is worthy of posterity.

WRITER'S BLOCK

The term 'writer's block' may be new to those for whom this is their first venture into the realm of 'creative writing' but it can be like a particularly nasty virus that strikes suddenly, laying you low for a time and for no apparent reason. And one of the worst aspects of both is the fear that you will never recover. You always do, of course, but it helps to do something positive to speed up that recovery. (I'm not including under this 'umbrella' the block that stems from an unwillingness to write about a deeply emotional or traumatic experience or period in your life. To attempt to force yourself to commit that to paper would, I believe, be not only unwise but could have serious results. The operative word, here, is 'force'. However therapeutic it might be to write about such experiences, it must always be when you, yourself, feel ready to deal with them and only you will know when that is.)

Different writers have different methods for dealing with the phenomenon of writer's block and it is a question of finding whichever one suits you best. But here are some ways you might find useful for stimulating creativity on those days when your brain refuses to co-operate.

1. If you can't write (for whatever reason), then read anything of an autobiographical nature. It is certain to trigger off memories and re-activate your thought-processes. In a class or group, whenever someone reads out a piece of their life story, it is astonishing how often there is a response from others of 'Oh yes, I remember that. We used to do that, too.' Or, 'We had one of those, as well.' Your subconscious is a remarkable tool when it

comes to bringing to the surface of your mind things you had completely forgotten but which will add interest and colour to your work.

(This is true of any kind of writing. Reading in the same genre invariably sparks off ideas of your own, regenerating that buzz of excitement so necessary if you are to produce anything of worth.)

2. Make a list of memory-joggers of the kind suggested on page 27. You might find it even more helpful if you can pin them up on a wall, where you will keep seeing them throughout the day. Again, this gives the subconscious a chance to get to work even though you are unaware of it, at the time. If, for instance, you have decided to write up a particular episode and you're having to struggle to get it down on paper, it is probably wiser to put it to one side, for the moment, and try something else instead. Having a list of possible topics on hand means you won't be stuck for another to start on. Also, keeping a file with possible headings on separate sheets of paper on which you've jotted down odd notes, keywords or phrases as and when they've occurred to you will, at moments like this, prove to be invaluable. You will have, immediately to hand, the basis of another complete piece for your book.

3. Get out your box of memorabilia, or perhaps a photograph album, and leisurely browse through it. Don't tell yourself you *must* come up with an idea to write about, just indulge yourself in a spot of old-fashioned nostalgia. Again, I would be surprised if, unwittingly, it didn't trigger off another train of thought.

4. Sit quietly somewhere and picture in your mind's eye a member of your family, past or present, or a particular family gathering, perhaps, and think how you would describe him or her, or one of those present at that gathering, to a complete stranger. Even if that particular character was of no special significance in your life, the chances are something else will be sparked off.

5. Imagine you're writing a letter or you've just bumped

into a friend and are bursting to tell him or her about this particular episode or incident. (Remember the advice given to Monica Dickens by her publisher. Take a piece of paper and write: Dear so and so, and then begin with: Did I ever tell you about . . . Or: Hey, so and so, let me tell you about that time when . . . You might even find speaking it into a tape-recorder helpful, pretending you have an actual audience listening, though some find it too inhibiting.

6.   A number of famous writers (Hemingway was one), finish their writing stint in the middle of a paragraph so that, when they return to it the next day, their mind quickly picks up the thread again, thus reducing that awful 'blank page' syndrome most writers know only too well.

7.   Some writers say that, if they sit themselves down to the typewriter and write absolutely *anything*, maybe copying out a page or two from a book, it gets them going again. Some, too, will sit for hours, if need be, in front of blank sheet of paper, refusing to give up until they've got some words down. Whilst I think the former might well work for some, personally, I cannot imagine anything more depressing than the latter 'cure'.

8.   If you've tried one or more of the above 'cures' without success, maybe you've been trying too hard to coerce your memory and imagination. In this case, my advice would be to put it aside for a while and do something completely different, allowing your creative 'well' time to replenish itself. Keep reading autobiographies; keep a notebook handy in which you jot down any odd phrase, line of dialogue or idea that comes into your mind at whatever time of day or night and, eventually, something will start stirring again and you'll take up your pen or go back to your typewriter with renewed vigour and enthusiasm.

Fictional techniques to add colour to your story

RE-CREATING CHARACTERS

'I am a part of all that I have met.'

Tennyson

Throughout our lives, we have all met people who, in one way or another, influenced us greatly. It might be a parent or grandparent who had certain qualities that we admired and were determined to emulate as we grew up, or perhaps it was a schoolteacher who imbued us with a love of literature or set us on the path we were to follow ever after.

In works of fiction, it is most likely that the characters portrayed will be a composite of people whom the author has known in real life, or at least observed, but they will (or should) be unrecognisable as such. The main ones will also be rather larger than life in order to make them more appealing to our readers and because it is through them, through their eyes and actions, that the story unfolds.

In an autobiography the people you are describing actually existed and, therefore, you will not normally want to disguise them. However, there is one notable exception to this: the type of book which, whilst drawing largely on the author's own experiences and so categorised as autobiography, is none the less fictionalised, to some extent. These, being written with the

51

definite aim of finding a publisher and intended to entertain, will have introduced characters who are an amalgam and, therefore, not easily identifiable, for obvious reasons.

The similarity between autobiography and fiction lies in the techniques used to create, or depict, the characters on the page and in the fact that you will only want to introduce the more colourful and interesting ones. In an autobiography, they will be those who remain clearest in your memory and, in all probability, those, too, who most influenced you during your formative years, possibly unknowingly, and who thus added to the rich tapestry of your early life.

Take yourself back to childhood and think of those whose faces, words or actions are most readily conjured up in your mind. You may not recall exactly the clothes they wore or the words they spoke but you will have retained an *impression*. Now, make a list of all those who roughly fit into the above category (you can add to it, later, as you remember others, perhaps adding a descriptive phrase or two on which to build when you actually start writing). My own quick list would include:

Great-Aunt Louisa	slim, vital, dressed in the long black bombazine dress of bygone era, twinkling dark eyes, dancing a jig at 80 + years of age.
Miss O'Loughlin	schoolteacher, soft Irish brogue; two Irish setters; believed in fairies; encouraged me to read and write.
Johnny Smythe	Irish ostler caring for carthorses at farm at bottom of lane where I grew up and, unknowingly, instilled in me a love of horses.
Father	First World War survivor; taciturn; market gardener.
Aunt Sally	typical 'caring' spinster; seamstress who taught me to sew.
Aunt Eleanor	self-educated, encouraged reading and learning.

We all have a wide variety of characters who were either present throughout a large part of our young lives or who, though merely flitting through, still left behind an indelible memory because, in some way, they affected our future.

Next, think of one or two incidents that would help bring them to life for your reader. By doing this, by seeing them in an action-replay, so to speak, you will probably remember them more clearly than before.

Now we come to putting into practice the fictional techniques of characterisation. As has already been said, it's unlikely, at a distance of many years, that we will recall every detail with exactitude – but that doesn't matter. We can use our imagination. We know (or can find out) the sort of clothes worn at that particular period and can describe them accordingly. If what was *said* was important, we can reproduce it in essence because their actions are probably sharply in focus. But, if we are to hold our reader's interest, it is essential that we describe them so vividly that they almost leap off the page.

Names

In fiction, the choosing of a character's name is of prime importance. In real life, it is chosen for us and we have to put up with it, even though we may not like it. However, sometimes we prefer to be known by a nickname or sobriquet so that may be relevant to the character you are portraying. Although my aunt's name was actually Sarah, she was never known by anything other than Sal or Sally. If she had belonged to a different stratum of society, the latter would never have been used.

There are definite fashions in names, with certain ones being extremely popular during a particular period. Years ago, a boy would often be given his father's name which might have placed undue stress on him as he grew up, trying to follow in his father's footsteps. Or perhaps you were named after someone for a different reason. Because my mother greatly admired a young lady of her acquaintance called Nancy, she hoped that, by giving her daughter the same name might somehow influence her character. It must have been a sore disappointment to her when it became evident I didn't have the same sweet and charming disposition as my namesake.

Physical Appearance

Physical appearance gives definite clues as to someone's personality. For instance, looking back, did your grandfather seem to be always smiling while your grandmother's brow was permanently furrowed and her mouth drawn into a tight forbidding line as if she had all the cares of the world on her shoulders? Did your uncle have a bump on the bridge of his nose and the 'cauliflower' ears of a pugilist or someone always in a fight, in his youth? Or perhaps you came from a military family with the result that everyone automatically developed a ramrod stance.

Describing physical appearance enables the reader to see your characters more clearly, while the way in which you describe them demonstrates your skill as a writer. For example:

His hands were brown and rough, like old, cracked leather, through a lifetime spent working on the land. Day after day, he planted, hoed and picked the cabbages, carrots, turnips and lettuce, tying them into bundles with coarse twine before packing into crates and hosing down with water to keep them fresh during the journey to market.

Her ready smile seemed to hover on her lips, warming her dark brown eyes so that you never noticed the plainness of her features.

She would have been described as beautiful if she could have afforded to have her luxuriant black tresses cut and shaped in the current fashion and washed with good shampoo. Instead, they were dragged back into an unbecoming bun which was held in place by thick, ugly, metal hairpins, lathered once a week with cheap soap and crudely chopped by herself, whenever they grew too long to manage. And her skin would have been milk-white and soft to the touch if it had only been cared for with the expensive lotions and cosmetics used by those better off women in whose houses she laboured, daily.

Roald Dahl in his *Boy – Tales of Childhood*, devotes one chapter to the headmaster of his school, describing him thus: 'His name was Mr Coombes and I have a picture in my mind of a giant of a man with a face like a ham and a mass of rusty-coloured hair that sprouted in a tangle all over the top of his head.' He goes on to say that he remembers him as a giant in a tweed suit with a waistcoat, over which he always wore a black gown.

In *They Must Have Seen Me Coming* by Louise Brindley, one of the characters is described like this: 'She wore, instead of the usual flowered overall, a green crimplene dress with an enormous velvet bow draped across her ample bosom, and her hair was so dark, so glossy, and set in such rigid waves and curls, that I found myself staring at it. Could it be a wig, I wondered?'

In a few well-chosen words, these characters spring to life off the page – the mark of good characterisation.

Clothing

The clothes we wear make an obvious statement about us even though, to some extent, they will be dictated by the fashion or mores of the time. My Great-Aunt Louisa was a strong, independent, courageous woman who ran a genteel guesthouse in the smarter part of Liverpool, enabling her to bring up her two children after she was widowed. But she clung to the long skirts and high-necked blouses of pre-World War One society, long after they had been abandoned by most women, presumably in an attempt to create an aura of respectability. I well remember her once telling me, sternly, that I should cover my knees with my skirt now I was six years old!

The person who dresses in gaudy colours is surely begging to be noticed? If gloves and socks are neatly darned, garments meticulously pressed, ties always worn, even on informal occasions, we can safely deduce that those people are fastidious in all aspects of their personal life, not just their appearance. Whilst I certainly cannot remember that my great-aunt's gloves were darned and her clothes were clean and neat, if I want to make the reader *see* her clearly, I can use my imagination to add those small 'brush-strokes' to my description because they accord with my remembered impression of her. My childhood memories of my father are of his being dressed in old corduroy trousers tied round the ankle with a length of string. Invariably, in wet or cold weather, he would have on a shabby, discoloured gabardine raincoat, passed on by some well-to-do gentleman, and fastened around the waist with twine. And, if working outdoors in the rain, a piece of sacking would be knotted around his shoulders for added protection. He had one decent suit for Sundays, weddings and funerals, and fashion didn't come into the· equation. That one suit would have lasted all of twenty years. Brown with a thin pale stripe, I'm sure it must have been shiny with all that wear and dated in style.

Here is an illustration of how a character might be depicted:

If I had to use one word to describe my grandmother it would be 'neat'. It wasn't until I was grown up that I marvelled at how she had managed to keep herself so in that tiny house with no running water inside, no WC, no bathroom. And to bring up a family of six children, also, seems to me, now, to have been a minor miracle. But Grandmother Johnson had determination in abundance. Her stockings were mended so neatly that the darns were almost works of art. Trousers were patched until they consisted of little else but patches upon patches.

Mannerisms/Body Language

Was your mother forever plumping up cushions and flicking a duster around the room or did she kick off her shoes wherever she happened to be, push aside any toys, books or other paraphernalia cluttering up a chair and flop herself down, ready for a sociable chin-wag? Two totally different personalities would be shown by such actions. Did your great-aunt, perhaps, seat herself primly, hands folded on her lap? Again, add small 'brush-strokes' to your descrptions:

Great-Aunt Maud seemed moulded to the straight-backed chair in which she always sat.

Uncle Henry's stiff-legged gait was a legacy of the wound that had invalided him out of the army during the First World War.

Character Traits

Remember not to *tell* us the sort of person someone was but *show* their character in action, either directly by means of a scene or indirectly as illustrated below. Just saying your grandfather was a generous man doesn't bring him to life for your reader.

My grandfather's generosity of spirit was a sore trial to my grandmother throughout her life. It was she who had to find, from somewhere, another coat to replace the one he'd given, without a second thought, to the old tramp he'd discovered sleeping under the hedge, shivering with cold. Or to stretch their meagre meal to fill an extra mouth when he brought home someone he thought in need of a meal.

Action

Showing a character in action is an excellent way of letting your reader see them as you once did.

> Johnny Smythe was a short, wizen-faced Irishman who spent all his days and nights with his beloved 'gentle giants', those huge shires that pulled the heavy drays, piled high with market garden produce, to market. Many were the hours I spent watching him grooming them till their coats gleamed like copper, neatly plaited manes emphasising the curve of their powerful necks, the featherings around their fetlocks shining like spun silk, the muscles in his wiry arms corded, sweat oozing through his worn checked shirt as he worked.

Remember to use energetic action verbs, whenever possible, which enable you to dispense with adverbs for added emphasis. For example, words like strode; limped; raced; grabbed; pummelled are stronger and more descriptive than saying; he walked quickly; he hit me hard.

Never forget the truism that *people are interested in people.* Thus, the more interesting and colourful characters you introduce into your autobiography, the more likely it is that your readers will enjoy it.

Exercise: Write a character sketch in which you describe physical appearance, show traits in action, include a short anecdote and some dialogue.

The following is a good example of character-drawing:

St Joe – Martyr by Margaret Finch

How he would have hated to know I had called him that! Partly because he was a devout Methodist and, as far as I know, they don't go in for all that saint business. But mainly because that would have been the last way he would have described himself.

58

We first met Joe D. around 1950 when he came to offer to help in the garden. He was a small, frail, old man, about eighty-ish, we thought, with twinkling eyes and a smile as sweet as a set of over-large, badly-fitting false teeth would allow. He rubbed his thigh continuously as he explained that 'a bit more brass comin' in were always welcome, as a pension didn't go all that far nowadays.'

From the look of him we did not expect too much, but any help was better than none on this neglected old property on the Yorkshire moors into which we had recently moved. How wrong we were! He limped off down the cobbled drive and, in next to no time, had scraped the weeds away from between the stones, the water-trough at the gate began to look a little more hygienic and he converted the old barn into a very respectable garage. Later, he dealt expertly with sickly hens and a request for a table-bird produced, within an hour, a plucked, dressed and still-warm corpse.

All the time he worked, he kept us entertained, in his thin reedy voice, interspersed with a laugh like a witch's cackle, with stories of the village folk. And all in a very broad country-Yorkshire accent which he took great delight in exaggerating, as he told me years later, for the pleasure of seeing our puzzled Lancastrian faces as we tried to work out what he was talking about.

We often wondered why he rubbed his leg so much. Then, one cold day as he crouched over the fire in his cottage, he answered my unspoken question. 'Shrapnel,' he said, suddenly, between the rubs. 'I were only a youngster and hadn't 't'sense to get out o' t' road. Ee, I were in 'ospital for months being mucked about. Deeper they dug for it, deeper it went in. Then they put a silver plate in me back. I'll bet tha didn't know I were worth a bit!' He cackled reminiscently. ''Ad a bit o' fun with them nurses, too. Ay, but it were a long time ago, '14 – '18 war, tha knows.'

59

He stopped and caught his breath as a particularly violent spasm seemed to overcome him for a moment. His wife, a tall, patient-looking woman took up the story. 'It's the cold, you know. He's always worse in winter. I don't know how many pairs of pants he goes through, rubbing that leg. Mind, they give him a bit extra on his pension for new ones, and I mend them as best I can but . . .' She shrugged her shoulders with a sigh. 'You wouldn't think he were only fifty-eight, would you?'

This little white-haired old man only fifty-eight? 'Aye,' she continued sadly, seeing the look on my face. 'He's been in pain for over thirty years, now. But as long as he can have his few sheep and hens round him, he's happy. He used to be a farmer – great strapping lad he were when we were wed. Now, well, he makes a bit with his woodwork when he can. Pension don't seem so big now as it did at first, even though t' lads have grown up and gone. Then there's our Len's Patsy to be looked after since her mother died.'

We had heard young Patsy – 'Eh, Grandad, will you mend me doll, its leg's come off?' Nothing was too much trouble for his beloved granddaughter.

One thing Joe revelled in was haunting the country cottage auction sales in the hopes of getting 'summat for naught'. Perhaps an old harmonium for five bob or, as a gift from a grateful autioneer, a chest of drawers which otherwise would have to be abandoned and left outside to rot. He would return from the day's outing gleefully rubbing his hands as he went in search of his woodworking tools. Within a day or so, the first coffee-table or some undefinable knick-knack would make its appearance to be bought by some kindly friend. We still have a magazine rack made from a couple of feet of mahogany grandfather-clock and topped by a lid which we suspect started life as part of an oak harmonium. He was so proud of it, I remember, especially when we assured him it was worth every penny of the pound or two we offered him for it.

We felt sure that each bitter Pennine winter would be his last as the cold penetrated his pain-racked leg and his face became a little greyer each day. But every spring found him sitting on an old bench in the sunshine, cheerfully whittling away at a piece of wood, rubbing his leg and thanking God to be still alive.

I don't know how many more winters he managed to survive as it is now several years since we left Yorkshire and lost touch with our old friend. But I do know that, on November 11th when I buy a poppy, it is Joe and his wife that I remember. And it is for them, and the others like them, that the two minutes of silent prayer is offered in gratitude and humility.

© Margaret Finch. Previously published in the *Huddersfield Daily Examiner.*

Note how quickly we get to know Joe in a few, well-chosen words. We learn he is a devout Methodist, is frail in build, looks much older than his years, has twinkling eyes, over-large false teeth and a permanent limp. He has a thin, reedy voice with a cackling, ever-ready laugh.

Dialogue introduces a touch of dialect but not so much that it becomes tedious and intrusive, using words and phrases peculiar to the region. For example, 'summat for naught'; 'a bit more brass' and the use of 'were' instead of the more grammatical 'was'.

DIALOGUE

A.E. Coppard once said that a character doesn't come to life until he speaks, which is an undoubted truism. If an incident or episode was of sufficient importance for you to want to relate it, then you will also need to include dialogue. Although, at a distance of maybe decades, it's unlikely you will be able to remember the exact words someone said, you will probably recall the flavour and tone of the words –

and that is all that matters. Indeed, in a TV interview, writer and playwright John Mortimer confessed that he no longer remembered which were the things his father had actually said and which were the bits of dialogue he had made up for his autobiographical play *Voyage Around My Father*. He said that fact and fiction become blurred in the memory.

However, as with a work of fiction, dialogue should only be included if it fulfils specific functions. In that way, it also increases the pace of the unfolding story, enlivens it and improves the actual appearance of the printed page by breaking chunks of narrative. In fiction, these functions are:

- To move the story forward;
- To help characterise;
- To provide necessary information.

In an autobiography, it is mainly the last two that need to be considered.

We learn a lot about someone from the way they speak. We can tell, for instance, if they have had only limited education because then they are likely to speak ungrammatically. They may say: 'It wasn't me that done it' or 'I'm going to have a lay down, now'. If they tend to be formal and 'stiff-necked', they will speak in that same manner, perhaps not using contractions. Instead of saying I didn't; I won't: you shouldn't, for example, they may say: I did not think you would do such a thing; I will not be long; you should not go there until you are given permission.

Thus, if you are describing your grandfather and you put into his mouth the following words: ''Ere, where d'you think you're off to, young fella-me-lad?' I think we can safely deduce he's a friendly sort of chap not given to standing on ceremony.

Dialogue is also a useful way of giving readers information

they need to have rather than in long passages of narrative. Suppose, for instance, you want to let us know that your favourite teacher, the only one to whom you could relate and who seemed to understand you when the others treated you like an irritating, stupid child, had suddenly left. You could tell us in straight narrative, writing:

> Miss Thomas was the only teacher I had ever really liked and got on with. She was always kind and patient and never seemed to mind however long it took me to stammer through my reading book. And when I went to school, one morning, and learned she'd suddenly left, I burst into tears, knowing school would never be the same again.

Or, you could make a scene of it, introducing dialogue:

> Miss Thomas was the only teacher I had ever really liked and got on with. Whenever I was attempting to stammer through the next page of my reading book she never lost patience but would say, 'Just take your time, Patricia. There's no hurry.' And she would flash me a sympathetic smile, as if she truly understood my fears of seeming stupid, my wish to sink through the floor when my words wouldn't come out properly. I suppose I thought she'd be there forever, the one friendly face in the whole place so, when I arrived at school, that day just before my ninth birthday in June, I was totally unprepared for what happened.
>
> Tom Fenton, one of the bigger boys from the top class, sauntered up to me as I entered the playground, gave me a shove then said with a snigger, 'So who'ye going to tell of me, now, Pat Johnson? 'Cos you're not going to be teacher's pet, anymore, are ye?'
>
> I opened my mouth to retort, then closed it again as I tried to make sense of what he'd said. At last, I faltered, 'What d'you mean?'
>
> 'I mean your old Miss Thomas has left, that's what. Didn't you know?' he jeered, seeing the horrified look on

my face. 'Me Dad told me she got the push. No good as a teacher. Only for stupid things like you.'

I felt the tears well up into my eyes as, stunned, I tried to take in what he was saying. At first, I refused to believe it but when, at assembly, the headmaster announced that Miss Thomas had, indeed, left and that a new teacher would be taking her place, the following week, the tears began to fall and I wept uncontrollably for most of that morning. And school, for me, was never the same again.

Because this was an important episode in your childhood, it warrants being expanded in this way. It might also be that Tom Fenton didn't actually exist; that he's largely a figment. of your imagination. But, as a means of adding colour and texture to this particular part of your story, it is legitimate to invent him. What you are doing is using fictional techniques to highlight that part of your story; to make it that bit more entertaining for your reader.

It also helps paint a picture of the sort of school you went to because Tom Fenton spoke ungrammatically and, doubtless, he wasn't the only one who did so. And there would probably have been a boy like him who did frighten you, at times. We will also learn that your early schooldays, at least, were an ordeal and our interest in what happened, later, will have been aroused.

A few words of action, using colourful verbs, will add to the description of how someone is speaking. For instance: '"Come 'ere, ye young tyke," Grandfather roared, shaking his walking stick at me, his normally placid face contorted with anger.' From this, the reader will gain more of a picture of the scene unfolding before him.

Be chary of using dialect too often or it will become tedious. If it is appropriate to include it, only introduce a few words. You can create the 'flavour' of a region by using words and phrases peculiar to it. Winifred Foley, in *A Child in the Forest*, employed both methods. ' . . . Dad scratched his head and observed with impartial dignity to Mam, "Mother 'tis a great pity thee 'asn't got my brains, or I 'asn't got thy energy, then one on us coulda' come to summat." '

The way dialogue is set out on the page is also important, especially if you intend trying to sell any or all of your book. The following short extract, from a very entertaining autobiography by Faith Addis entitled *The Year of the Cornflake*, serves to illustrate this. It also, I think, makes the point about letting your imagination supply the words someone used because I doubt that the author remembered the exact ones. You will note that each time a different person speaks, a new paragraph is begun. The purchase of a cow is being discussed:

> 'It is legitimate. It's perfectly *legitimate* to describe a seventeen-year-old cow as a seven-year-old cow, but it's not right, is it?'
>
> 'Seventeen? But Reg said . . .'
>
> 'Reg saw you coming did Reg. 'Tisn't every day a farmer gets a chance to sell a pup. Couldn't resist it, could he?'
>
> 'How do you *know* Bambi is seventeen?'
>
> Tony looked at me pityingly. 'Quite *apart* from the fact that Bambi wears her udder round her ankles' – he paused to let this shaft sink in – 'and quite *apart* from the fact that she's got no flesh on her, I happen to have seen her around for at least twelve years, and the old lady that owned her bred her herself in 1959 or thereabouts.'

Finally, there are three good reasons for including plenty of dialogue in your book:

- It makes for easier reading than huge tracts of straight narrative.
- Its adds pace and immediacy.
- It makes the actual printed page more attractive to the eye.

Thus, let your characters speak as often as possible and you will make your book that much more enjoyable and, therefore, likely to be successful.

Exercise: Write a scene between two characters who are either (a) vehemently disagreeing over something or (b) saying goodbye, expecting never to see each other again. Use as little narrative and as few speech tags as possible (he said; she replied; he retorted; and so on) and make sure each character speaks quite differently from the other.

DESCRIPTIONS

Using the Five Senses

It is important that you convey a sense of place to your reader and the way to do that is through the use of the five senses: sight, sound, smell, taste and touch. It is all too easy to forget that scenes which are indelibly etched on your own mind will not be equally clear in the reader's *unless you make them so by your writing*. So, take yourself back in time and ask yourself questions:

1. What was the weather like at the particular time you're describing? Was it hot and sunny or overcast with storm clouds? Did the sun seem to shine out of a clear blue sky every single day throughout that summer? Was the grass parched and dry or lusciously green? Were the roads dusty, rutted with cart tracks, littered on either side with rubbish?

    What were the people around you like – dark-skinned, the men's heads swathed in soiled white cotton turbans, the women in colourful saris? Were there beggars clad only in rags, holding out begrimed bony hands for a few coins? Were the children bare-foot and dressed in patched and worn clothing?

2. Unless you were in the middle of nowhere, there must have been a variety of sounds around you. Try to describe them so that your reader can hear them, too. The shrill bugle call rousing the soldiers each morning; the blast of the ship's siren as it edged away from the quay; the wailing of the women as news of the disaster spread; the mournful cry of the curlews as the waves crashed against the shore; the plaintive bray of the donkey in the field beside the house; the musical soughing of the wind in the trees. Let these and other sounds echo again in your mind and stir perhaps long-forgotten memories.

3. Smell is supposed to be the most evocative of all the senses, yet it is probably the least drawn upon when writing descriptive passages. I once remember reading a tip from an estate agent for making one's house seem more attractive to a potential buyer: it was to put some coffee on to percolate. Why? Because the aroma would create a feeling of comfort, of homeliness, of *caring*. Why do women wear perfume if not to create a specific sense of personality, of glamour, sophistication, elegance or, depending on the scent used (rose water or eau de cologne, for instance), perhaps one of motherliness, of simplicity and reassurance?

    Anyone who has travelled in the East could not fail to have been aware of the powerful smells, especially in the bazaars, arising from the spices, fruits, cooking food, incense burning. Somehow, you must re-create all of this for those who have never had that same experience or they will not be able to fully enter into your world.

4. Taste can be a very individual thing because we all have our own likes and dislikes. None the less, if you can conjure up in your reader's mind the taste of mouth-burning curry, of tangy fresh oranges, palate-cleansing watermelon, you will have added another dimension to your writing.

5. For those without sight or hearing, touch must play a

67

very large part in their lives and perhaps those of us more fortunate tend to forget its importance to us all. So, when you are describing a place or an incident, try to recall how everything *felt* – the searingly hot, sand-laden wind on your skin; the smooth bark of the tree trunk beneath your fingers, the cold heavy weight of the gun on your shoulder.

Brush Strokes

When your description is down on paper, remind yourself it is only the first draft and, whether you go over it straight away or leave it until later when you start to revise, you will evoke the atmosphere, bring it more to life for others, if you add a few vital 'brush-strokes'. In the same way as an artist highlights and emphasises his painting by a few swift touches of his brush, so, too, will they make all the difference to your text. For example, if your mother's eyes were blue, what *kind* of blue were they, exactly?

'My mother's eyes were blue as the periwinkles that grew in our tiny cottage garden'? Or: 'My mother's eyes were like the sky on a clear winter's day'?

'A wind was blowing through the trees on that particular day in the spring of 1928' – but what sort of wind and what kind of trees were they?

'A piercing, icy wind blew through the copse of silver birches that early spring day in 1928.' (Do you see how much sharper the image is in the latter version?)

'The view above the harbour was breathtaking.' That tells us very little about the view, apart from allowing our imagination to perhaps fill the harbour with boats. Tell it like this, and we learn a great deal more: 'Standing on the steep, grassy slope above the harbour, I caught my breath at the picture spread out below, white sails blowing in the strong westerly breeze, the sinking sun touching the masts with gold.'

Let's now take a look at each of the five senses and how,

recalling specific objects, they take us on a magic carpet to the past.

Sight The colour and shape of things often need to be described, especially if they are likely to be unfamiliar to most of your readers. Remember those yellow sticky strips of fly-paper we used to hang in strategic places before the advent of sprays? And the wire-net fly-swats that left horrible squashed black bodies over the windows? It's many years since I've seen either of those once common household items.

Don't be afraid of describing in too much detail: that's almost impossible.

Sound Music, birdsong, wind, storm, sea, traffic, animal calls, church bells. Specific sounds have the power to recall, instantly, certain memories. Hearing raised voices shouting, arguing and haggling, issuing from the bazaar made me think of the Tower of Babel and, over and above it all, at certain times of the day, floated the disembodied wail of the muezzin from the minaret of the nearby mosque as he called the Faithful to prayer.

In order to recreate for your reader certain sounds you may find the use of metaphor or simile effective. Ruth Rendell is a master at this. For example: 'Her voice was like the clattering of bin-lids'.

Smell Remember that this is the sense most often overlooked and try to introduce it whenever you can. Many things which were once common household smells no longer are. For example, mothballs, lavender bags, black-lead, carbolic soap, baking bread, nutmeg and other spices used in cake-making, camphorated oil, eau de cologne and so on. Add to this list from your own memories.

Touch The bark of a tree, materials such as velvet and silk, warm flesh, rough, work-hardened skin. Don't forget to include touch in your descriptions, it will add to the picture you are building.

Taste   The sharp tang of fresh lemons just picked from the tree; the curry so hot it made you gasp and your eyes water; the tingle on your tongue of fizzy 'ginger-pop'.

Your descriptions should be vivid enough to evoke a sense of place so that your reader is *there* with you. Christabel Bielenberg, in *The Past is Myself*, her graphic account of her life in Germany during the Second World War, painted the following picture of one wartime Christmas.

> It was snowing outside, big white flakes that melted when they touched the windows. It was all so unreal. Behind me, in the sitting room, that Christmas tree should not be standing bulkily in the corner, covered with cotton wool, but right in the middle of the room, covered with sweets and lametta and gyrating slowly, a trifle jerkily, on its little silver stand, which had turned the tree when Peter's grandfather was a boy. The room should not be tidy and smelling of cigar smoke, but strewn with Christmas paper, and the air should be filled with the pungent smell of gingerbread and candle grease, which every German child associates only with Christmas.

Exercise: Write up an early memory, drawing on all five senses to add colour to your piece, to give the reader a sense of place.

SHOW, DON'T TELL: INDIRECT EXPOSITION OR WRITING IN SCENES

'Show, don't tell' is an expression often bandied about in writers' groups of all kinds. It is also an exhortation that the new writer finds it difficult to fully understand and put into practice. But it is one of those various tools of the writer's trade, a piece of fictional technique, it is important to use in order to bring a particular scene to life.

In fact, all it really means is – don't *tell* an important bit of your story in straight narrative but make a scene of it so that we *see* it happening, rather as if it were unrolling before our eyes on screen or stage. It is *showing* your characters in action rather than *telling* us what they were like. But examples are much the best way to get a point across so I hope the following will help you understand the concept. The first piece is the wrong approach.

Telling

My grandfather had lived with us for as long as I could remember and I adored him, though he was often the bane of my mother's life. He frequently took himself off for long walks and, as a small child, whenever I saw him leaving the house, I would run after him and beg him to let me come, too. He could be very sharp-tempered, I remember, and he and my mother had many arguments because she also was inclined to be waspish. But he was also a great story-teller (he was an old liar, according to my mother) and I loved to hear his stories about his life in the army in the war.

We learn a good deal about the grandfather from the above piece but we don't actually *see* him arguing, going for long walks, telling fascinating tales of army life to his young grandson. Clearly, he was a very influential part of the author's childhood and so will occupy a prominent place in his autobiography.

Showing

My grandfather had lived with us for as long as I could remember and I adored him, though he was often the bane of my mother's life. Probably because of the constant

71

arguments between them, he frequently took himself off for long walks, walks on which, whenever possible, I tried to accompany him. Etched sharply on my memory are the many times when I begged him to let me come, too.

'Please, Grandpa,' I cried in a plaintive voice, 'can I come with you? I'll be ever so good, I promise. And I'll sit outside The Lamb as quiet as anything,' I added slyly, knowing from experience that the pub in the next village was his favourite watering hole and stopping place.

Grandpa grunted a sigh of reluctant agreement as he took his ancient ash walking-stick from its peg in the hall. 'But you'd best behave yourself, young man,' he admonished, wagging a gnarled finger at me, his thick white eyebrows meeting in a stern frown. 'And don't you be telling your mother where we went or she'll be starting on me, again, saying I'm a bad influence on you.'

I shook my head, vehemently. 'I promise, Grandpa. Cross my heart.'

'Right. Come on, then, boy. Stop dallying about. Let's go, if we're going,' he barked, pulling on his old cloth cap. And, without waiting to see if I was following, he opened the door, strode down the narrow garden path and was out into the lane beyond, his long legs covering the ground as easily as if he were half his age, leaving me running, breathlessly, to catch up with him.

Using this same technique, the story can continue with the author struggling to keep up with his grandfather, letting us see how, whilst pretending to be irritated, every now and then the old man stops to look over a field gate. The child can start him off on one of his favourite tales by saying something like: 'I bet you never drove a tank, did you, Grandpa?' thus allowing an opportunity to have Grandpa relate, briefly, an anecdote from the war.

The next example is an extract from Chapter 14 of *Diana's Story*, the poignant but often humorous account by Deric Longden of how he and his wife, Diana, coped with her crippling illness. I think you will see the way in which we discover a great deal about his mother through action and dialogue: through being *shown*.

My mother put the first-aid box back on the shelf and pulled out the knife drawer.

'They'll not be in there – I keep them in here.' In my innocence I had thought that a first-aid box was the natural place to keep an aspirin, but I was wrong.

'That's for plasters and things – you don't keep aspirins in there.' She laid out first the forks on the draining-board and then the spoons. 'They're in here somewhere.' The knives followed, and then the larger spoons and ladles until the drawer was empty. She was puzzled. 'I could have sworn they were in here.' And then a great beam came over her face.

'How silly of me – I had a clear out,' and with a confident air she opened the butter compartment in the fridge door and produced a single soluble aspirin.

From this passage, and as it continues in the same vein, it is quite obvious that the mother is well-intentioned but not very efficient, one of those delightfully vague people who are lovable but difficult to live with.

Exercise Take any incident you intend including in your life story and write it up in narrative form. Then re-write using the 'show, don't tell' method, remembering to introduce dialogue and action. When you've mastered this technique, you will be well on the way to writing a lively, entertaining autobiography.

73

EMOTION

'Strong emotion must leave its trace.'

Virginia Woolf

If you are an unknown and serious about trying to get your autobiography published, *moving* your readers is essential. Indeed, Paul Gallico, that master of wringing the heartstrings, said: 'To sell, you only have to capture the imagination and *touch the human heart.*' (Italics mine) But, above all, you must move them to laughter, or at least bring a smile to their lips.

I think it is true to say that most of the autobiographies by 'ordinary' people which have been very successful have been humorous in style and content, though they have possessed other qualities as well, including warmth and compassion, and have provided an insight into a life-style vastly different to that of most of us.

I well remember laughing out loud in a hotel lounge whilst reading one of Lilian Beckwith's 'Hebridean' series, then glancing round, embarrassed, hoping no one had heard me! James Herriot's popular 'vet' books described situations calculated to amuse without being heavy-handed, which is always a danger when one deliberately sets out to be funny. A successful writer of women's fiction once said to me: 'The reader loves to cry.' I think she was right – but we don't want to be depressed, which is quite another thing. Ideally, we should aim to create a balance of tensions by bringing moistness to the eye one minute, a smile to the lips the next. A mixture of humour and pathos is a sure-fire recipe for success, as has been demonstrated time and again by many writers and none more so than by Deric Longden in his moving account of his wife's long battle against illness, *Diana's Story.*

But, just as humour should spring naturally from a situation and not be forced into it, so, too, the sad parts should not be excised from your story. In *Lost For Words*, Deric Longden's sequel to his first book, describing his life following Diana's death, he tells of how he began to write *Diana's Story*, using material previously written for radio, and how the literary agent, June Hall, met him for lunch to discuss it with him. After chatting for a while, he says June Hall '. . . patted my fifty pages of tarted-up radio scripts – all filleted for easy reading. "So where's the pain?" she asked.'

He goes on to explain how, up until then, he had painted word-pictures in light colours to hide the reality, picking out the humour in pastel shades – never dipping into the black. June Hall told him, 'If you can do it – you'll have a book.' And he drove home 'to write the pain'. The result became a best-seller.

To quote one of our most famous authors, Catherine Cookson, 'The aim of the writer should be to touch the heart of the reader.' In her autobiography, *Our Kate*, she told of growing up as the illegitimate (what an out-dated word that is, now!) child of an alcoholic mother whom she thought was her sister, a story which could not fail to move the most stony-hearted reader.

Recalling some of the most riveting pieces read out by students in class, I asked myself what it was they had in common – and the answer was: emotion. Sometimes they made us laugh out loud or at least grin at each other. Sometimes the tale unfolding was so horrifying, so gripping, that no one moved a muscle or made a sound. At other times, eyes became moist and, on one never-to-be-forgotten occasion, everyone single person sitting around that table was visibly struggling to hold back the tears. That was the only occasion when I, too, had to reach for my handkerchief because, normally, as the tutor and leader of the group, I need to remain detached and objective.

Once, a young woman, her voice and hands shaking, related an account of what must surely have been the worst moment in her whole life. Married to a violent and jealous husband, she finally decided to leave him, taking her small son with her. Suitcase in one hand and clasping her son with the other, she set off down the garden path while her husband threatened them with a shotgun from the window behind. An almost tangible chill permeated the room as we listened and empathised, both with the author during that terrifying incident and for her courage in recounting such a shocking experience to a roomful of strangers. Except that, by then, we were no longer really strangers. As a group, over the weeks and months, we had welded together through mutual trust, vicariously sharing each other's experiences of grief and tragedy, love and hope, joy and awe.

Another time, a recently retired doctor wrote of an experience that had obviously seared itself across his mind and soul for nearly fifty years. As a very young soldier in the army medical corps, at the end of the last war, he had been posted to Germany and found himself at Belsen where he stayed and worked for several weeks. He was from a devoutly religious family, and it needed little imagination on our part to understand the difficulty of coming to terms with what he saw there and retaining his faith. The effect of that piece of autobiographical writing was made even more poignant for all of us by the coincidence of its being read out just before eleven o'clock on the morning of Armistice Sunday.

A friend, having just learned that her husband had been unfaithful and that her marriage was at an end, and also being a writer, sat down and wrote an account of her discovery and how she *felt* at the betrayal and her grief at the break-up of their many years together. Later, she told me that, when she sent it off to a women's magazine, which was inviting personal experiences, the paper was still wet and stained with the tears she had shed whilst writing it.

Whatever the reason for the revelations of these writers, their stories were told straight from the heart and I believe they *needed* to be told. I have little doubt that, reaching down into the well of their own emotion and pouring it out on paper would have proved cathartic, helped them come to terms with events in their lives, events which may have been too painful ever to talk about, before.

Don't be afraid of expressing your deepest feelings on paper, thinking you might be accused of going 'over the top'. There is always an unavoidable gap between how you, the writer, feel as you're putting it down and how it comes across to the reader. Letting us know how you *felt*, at the time, is an important part of vividly recreating a scene or incident for your audience. To help with this, you might find it useful to make a list of words that convey that particular feeling, words that will conjure up relevant images in the mind of the reader or listener. For example, suppose the main emotion (the *tone*) you want to bring out in your piece is fear, list any words that spring to mind which have any sort of connection with it, words that might add to the pervading atmosphere: for example, shiver; tremble; shake; palpitate; sweat; shadow; darkness; creak. There must be many more, so just keep adding them as you think of them.

It isn't necessary to do this at the moment of actual creation, unless you wish to. It may well be better left until you come to the rewriting, either after each separate piece or chapter or when you've finished the entire book. Everyone will find their own best working method but words are the tools with which every writer has to work and choosing the right ones will undoubtedly enhance your work.

Tolstoy once said that: 'Real art depends first on feeling.' Thus any writer who can master the ability to *move* the reader is well on the way to becoming not just a craftsman but a true artist. And a successful one.

Exercise Emotions experienced during childhood can often remain powerful and raw throughout our lives. Take yourself back through the years to when you were very young and try to recall a particularly happy, painful or sad event or incident which reawakens in you strong and perhaps still unresolved feelings. Write it up exactly as you remember it, placing as much emphasis as possible on how you *felt* at the time.

In Section 6 of this book, you will find a piece entitled 'Incident from an Australian Childhood' in which the author describes an occurrence on her seventh birthday which she has never forgotten – nor, clearly, completely forgiven. It is a good example of emotion recollected and examined, many years later.

CONFLICT

If I had to choose just one vital ingredient needed to make a piece of fiction successful, it would be *Conflict* – 'No conflict, no story' is a wise maxim to keep in mind. While a life story is somewhat different, none the less, it is the problems and difficulties, the clashes with parents, siblings, friends and 'authority', the inner battles with conscience, with desire, fear, envy and so on that make for gripping reading.

It is this that will add the necessary spice to your life story, if you are to hold your reader's interest. You've included colourful characters, described beautiful, exotic or drab surroundings and ensured your dialogue is realistic. You've organised your material and structured your book so that it falls into a logical sequence. You've introduced action and written in scenes, where appropriate. But, if there isn't also plenty of conflict to add interest and piquancy, the mixture will be too bland and your book will be as flat and unexciting to read as an unseasoned meal would be to eat.

You may dislike conflict in your own life and wish it did not exist but the plain fact is that, however lamentable, it is a part of our daily diet through the media and I suspect we would soon stop buying newspapers or watching the news on TV if they only reported pleasant happenings. But it does not have to involve physical or even verbal violence. There are actually three types of conflict (useful to know if, later, you decide to try your hand at fiction), any or each of which you should try to bring into your autobiography. These are:

- Man against man;
- Man against nature;
- Man against himself.

When selecting your material, if wise, you will have omitted the duller bits, those periods when everything went comparatively smoothly. This should ensure that, throughout most of your book, you will automatically have included plenty of conflict. Don't let the word itself put you off. Remember, it doesn't mean only major, fight-to-the-death, dramatic struggles against flood or famine or the law, for example, but it must be there, in some form or other, illustrating your fight to overcome both the large and the small problems that life hands out to us all.

Take the example of the grandfather, living with his daughter and family, and his small grandson (fictionalised, though based on an actual people). The boy's loyalty is constantly being torn in two, adoring his grandfather, lapping up his wonderful, exaggerated tales of derring-do yet conscious of how the old man irritates his long-suffering mother. Think of the friction constantly being generated in that household.

If, on the other hand, all had been sweet harmony, it could have been covered in a few words: 'My grandfather came to live with us when I was very small and so was a part of my growing up. He fitted into our household as if he'd always been there, easy-going, amenable and loved by us all until the day he died.' You might have gone on to say something about how he tended the garden, slept every afternoon and described his physical appearance, but he wouldn't have the same appeal to your potential readers as would an often cantankerous, sometimes generous, always fascinating old rogue, though doubtless much easier to live with.

If you have had a really dramatic experience, of course,

this is a 'must' to include because don't we all love to live through these, vicariously, in the safety of our own home?

But what of battles with your conscience (man against himself)? Take this opportunity to let your family understand why you made certain decisions. Let them know about your desperate inner struggle before taking a particular action.

Were you in North Devon at the time of the devastating floods a few decades ago? Or living near to the Welsh coal-mining village of Aberfan at the time of that horrific slag-heap disaster? Did you grow up in another such village and, therefore, are able to graphically describe the effect of a pit disaster on the entire community? Or perhaps you were born by the sea and have memories of a dramatic lifeboat rescue.

Take every possible opportunity to introduce conflict into your life story and you will greatly increase your chances of finding, and keeping, an audience.

If you doubt what I'm saying, check it out for yourself. Take an analytical look at some of those successful autobiographies, noting where, when and how conflict is introduced, and I think you will be convinced. The following are examples, taken from various published autobiographies, in which the author found him or herself in a situation of conflict of varying degrees.

From *Travels with a Donkey* by R. L. Stevenson: Stevenson is travelling through the Cevennes with the donkey, Modestine, who is proving obstinate:

> 'A little out of the village, Modestine, filled with the demon, set her heart upon a by-road, and positively refused to leave it. I dropped all my bundles, and, I am ashamed to say, struck the poor sinner twice across the face. It was pitiful to see her lift up her head with shut eyes, as if waiting for another blow. I came very near crying . . .'

Apart from the external conflict with the donkey, there was also inner conflict as the author's conscience plagued him.

In *A Child in the Forest*, Winifred Foley graphically describes the terror of a young Winnie sent by her mother to get a joint of meat from the butcher after darkness had fallen. Her throat is tight with terror by the time she reaches the garden gate. She decides to walk down the middle of the rough cobbled path that surrounds the village, fearing that, if she keeps too near the dry-stone garden walls, weird-faced apparitions might pop up over them. And if she walks too near the ditched bank bordering the forest, she might be within arm's reach of the monsters and ogres hiding behind the trees.

In *Not Without My Daughter* by Betty Mahmoody, the author and her small daughter have been taken to Iran for a two-week holiday but are being kept there, unwillingly, while her Iranian husband is becoming violent.

> Angered by her defiance, Moody grabbed her hand and jerked her away from me roughly. At the same time, he kicked her sharply in the back.
>
> 'No!' I yelled at him. Encumbered by the heavy *chador*, I lunged after my daughter.
>
> Moody immediately turned his wrath upon me, screaming at the top of his lungs, spitting out every English obscenity he could recall. I began to cry, suddenly impotent against his rage.

Exercise Write up three episodes in your own life in which you were in conflict with

- another person;
- nature – with one of the elements, flood or fire, perhaps, or maybe with an animal such as a bull in a field or trying to rescue a wild or trapped creature;
- yourself – with your conscience or over a strong, ill-founded desire or fighting to conquer a desperate fear.

FLASHBACK

Flashback is another fictional technique that can sometimes be usefully employed in writing your life story. It is a device for explaining or showing something which occurred further back in the past than the period you are relating, something which affected the rest of your life, to a greater or lesser degree. (In fiction writing, flashback is often used to show the motivation for a character's actions for, without credible motivation, such actions will not be believable, either.)

A flashback is most commonly signposted by changing to the pluperfect tense (someone *had* done something), before moving back into the simple past tense (in which most of the narrative will be written) to describe the scene which immediately follows. The main reason for this is that too many 'hads' become cumbersome if constantly used.

The occasional use of flashback will also add variety to your story. It can help show how what is happening to you at one particular point of your life is affected by an event which took place years before in the more distant past. For example, suppose your granddaughter, who emigrated to Australia some time ago, wants you to fly out for her wedding but you've never flown before and you're terrified at the thought. At first, you think you'll refuse – and then you remember how, years ago, you almost didn't go somewhere else through fear, how you finally forced yourself to make the trip – and were always glad that you did. You did it once, you tell yourself, so you can do it again. The second time, overcoming what proved an irrational fear won't be so difficult.

Relating the incident might start like this:

When the airmail letter arrived bearing an Australian stamp, I knew, immediately, it was from my granddaughter, Gemma, and I tore it open as excitedly as if it were a birthday present. I loved my youngest grandchild dearly and had missed her more than I could say since she'd gone to live in Australia, three years ago. With trembling fingers, I took out the sheets of thin blue paper – and my heart sank as I began to read.

Gemma was getting married and wanted me to fly to Sydney for her wedding. Cost was no problem and, in any case, it seemed her fiancé had offered to pay for the flight. The problem was *fear*. I'd never flown before!

I couldn't possibly go, I told myself, at first. And then I remembered that other time, nearly thirty years earlier, when Edward had wanted me to visit him in France. Then, too, I had panicked and said 'No'. But I'd known my brother was desperately ill, maybe dying, and so, after much wavering, several stiff drinks and being almost forcibly put on the train by my eldest daughter, I had gone. (Notice the change of tense to the pluperfect – I *had* panicked; I *had* gone – before moving back to the simple past in the next bit.)

Edward was there to meet the cross-channel ferry at Calais and I knew I had been right to come. He looked so thin and yellow and wizened, though he was as bright and cheerful as I remembered. He took my arm and hailed a taxi to drive us to an hotel. And then began a wonderful and astonishing two weeks when I saw my brother in a totally new light. His courage was remarkable and, when we finally said 'Goodbye', I think we both knew we would never see each other again in this life.

I was always glad I had made that trip. If I had not, I would have regretted it for ever. (We've signalled the end of the flashback by returning to the pluperfect – I *had* made; If I *had* not – before recommencing the simple past.)

So now, re-reading Gemma's letter, I knew I must accept her invitation or I would always regret it. Because, I reminded myself, who knows what lies ahead for any of us?

In *Lost for Words*, Deric Longden's sequel to *Diana's Story*, he uses a neat stylistic flashback device. He introduces a few lines of dialogue, *using italics*, so that we know those words were spoken further back in time. For example, it is perfectly clear that the following conversation took place many years earlier, between his parents:

> *'Where do you think it would look best?'*
> *'In Deric's room – he'd be hurt if not.'*

Remember that flashback, like all fictional techniques, is merely another tool for making your writing more vivid and interesting to read. But, if you do use it, you must make it clear to your readers that the events you are describing occurred in the far distant past. If not, they will be confused, will have to re-read to make sense of it and may end up feeling irritated enough to stop reading at that point.

Exercise   Write up an incident in which you introduce a flashback (it can be quite brief) to the distant past, remembering to signal you are moving into it and out of it, again, by using the pluperfect tense.

TENSION

Tension is one of the most important elements in fiction-writing, closely allied to suspense – the 'what happens next' ingredient. If you can also introduce it into your autobiography, you will add an extra dimension in the entertainment stakes. Obviously, the reader knows you survived whatever traumas and dramatic events have occurred throughout your life but he doesn't know *how*. You developed TB/polio/diphtheria/were involved in a plane crash or whatever and, immediately, we want to know what followed, how you coped with the situation in which you found yourself. The secret is not to give it away too quickly. Keep us guessing, hanging on to every word, thus building up tension and suspense.

You've probably heard the saying, 'Make 'em laugh, make 'em cry, make 'em wait' (advice often given actors, too). It pithily sums up the essence of writing which is about *moving* the reader at the same time as persuading him to continue to turn the pages, to keep on reading. I think it was Joseph Conrad who commented that, in order to write a good story, one only needed to be able to keep the reader in suspense. This is because we want to be kept on tenterhooks, to be surprised and astonished. And as someone once put it, writing that has no surprises is as bland as oatmeal.

In order for there to be tension in your story, there must be (or have been) something important at stake. Perhaps this was your health or life or what you believed to be your future happiness. Perhaps it was your chosen career that hung in the balance. Or maybe you are describing a highly-charged incident, part of a particularly difficult period in your life. Whatever it was, by not divulging the outcome too soon, you will maintain your reader's interest for that much longer.

In *Not Without My Daughter*, the tension starts to build on the first page, while Betty Mahmoody and her little girl are still on the plane on the way to Iran for what is supposed to be a two-week holiday. She tells herself it was a mistake to go but had felt unable to refuse and believes she must trust her husband, Moody. Once in Iran, she finds herself being forced into accepting various demands made upon her by Moody and his family. She is told she must wear the drab, all-enveloping *chador* worn by all Iranian women. She asks if she would be arrested if she refused and is told, bluntly, 'Yes'. Thus, we start to wonder if she *will* be arrested, at some point in the story.

She finally learns her husband intends they shall stay in Iran forever and knows it is up to her to find a way to escape and get herself and Mahtob back to America. One morning, they manage to slip out of the house, unseen by Moody's family, and set out for the Swiss Embassy, which has a US Interest Section. The tension increases further as they hurry along intimidated by the hubbub of the bustling city and uncertain of which direction to go. Betty's heart pounds with fear, knowing they are committed and unable to gauge the ferocity of Moody's reaction once he realises they have fled. But she has no intention of returning and allows herself the faintest sigh of relief, believing they will never see him again. But of course, we know they will – otherwise the book might have ended there.

Words and phrases were obviously carefully selected to create a tense atmosphere and include: intimidated; heart pounded with fear; ferocity. Thus, tension and suspense were built up so that, metaphorically, we hold our breath, impelled to read on to find out 'what happens next'.

SECTION THREE

Article writing

STRUCTURING THE ARTICLE

If it's your autobiography you're engaged upon, you might wonder why I should suggest you also write some articles. In fact, there are several reasons why.

1. If your story is to be in short sections, some of them will be complete in themselves and may well be article-length and saleable as such.
2. If you are aiming to try and sell your book, being able to tell a prospective publisher that you've already had one or more short excerpts from it in print will prove to him you can write to a publishable standard.
3. Even if your actual book never reaches a wide audience, allowing others to share in a traumatic, dramatic, happy or sad experience may give comfort, hope or pleasure to not a few. Often, when we are going through a painful period in life, we feel very alone, believing that no one else has been through that particular experience and that it will never end. Reading about someone else who has been in the same situation – and come through it – can help break the sense of alonenness.
4. Last, but not least, having just one piece of writing accepted and *paid for* will give your self-confidence a

miraculous boost. Knowing that people out there will be parting with good money to read what *you* have written creates a glow like nothing else when you first start out. And, if you see your life story as merely the start of a whole new exciting phase, you will have set out on the right foot because there is no doubt that articles are easier both to write and to sell than fiction and the potential market is vast.

Let's take a look at each of the above reasons in greater depth.

If, in order to make your task less daunting, you've chosen to write your book in separate short sections, it will be a definite help to structure each section as if it were a complete article. In this way, you won't wander from one subject or one episode to another which would end up as a rambling, confused and confusing piece. And it is all too easy for this to happen unless you do organise and structure your work, as I've seen with students when they first approach their autobiography.

It is probably self-evident that the fact that an editor has accepted a piece of your work to appear in print is a good recommendation for any publisher to at least take a careful look at the rest of what you have produced.

In Section 6, you will find a moving true account of how someone coped with living with a terminal illness. The author was, himself, a doctor and so knew all the implications when he was diagnosed as having cancer. As just another human being having been given a virtual death sentence, however, he was as vulnerable and afraid as anyone else. But, by writing of his feelings, by telling of how he dealt with his fears and coped with getting on with life during the time he had left, he must have helped hundreds, if not thousands, of others. And, perhaps, by some of that account being reproduced in this book, he will have extended the range of that help more than he could ever have thought possible.

In my file of published pieces by some of my students, I have another touching piece by a woman who had to make the agonising decision to place her elderly mother in a home when her senile dementia (Alzheimer's disease) became too much for the daughter to cope with. It was a heartrending plea for forgiveness, written after her mother had mercifully died and, I'm sure, helped resolve her feelings of guilt. But, undoubtedly, it would have struck a chord in the heart of many others in the same situation and helped them realise they were not alone in such a terrible dilemma and perhaps come to the same difficult decision.

Similarly, another tells of how she joined a dating agency and found her 'prince charming' who, by a total coincidence, lived in the same town. A message of hope to others that happiness can lie just around the corner if you do something positive about trying to find it. Each of these, surely, fulfilled a worthy purpose in being printed in magazines that would reach a much wider audience than just the few dozen or so of immediate family?

I have seen, over and over again, a budding writer's self-confidence grow after just one acceptance. This is especially true, I might add, of women who, unless they have had careers of their own, frequently see themselves only as extensions of their husbands. So many times have I heard, when asking students to introduce themselves at the start of a new class, women members say, diffidently: 'Oh, I haven't done anything, really. I'm only a housewife.' And to see them blossom and grow when, perhaps many weeks later, they see that what they have written is not only being taken seriously but is often considered worthy of being in print, is something wonderful to behold. And when a piece actually is accepted and they hold the letter, and sometimes the cheque, too, in their hands, the change in them is astonishing. Their writing, from then on, flows more freely and increases in strength and they begin to think in terms of achieving a previously undreamed of success.

Now, having discussed *why* one should consider writing one's life story in separate article-sized chunks, let us look at *how* to structure them. At this point, I would ask you to think visually, take a pen and draw a large diamond shape, which is how I see the structural shape of an article. You can use this diagram to ensure that each separate section (whether you're aiming to try and sell it or not) is soundly constructed so that it 'hangs together' as a complete whole. I would suggest, too, that you put it into practice by deciding on one specific incident or theme and writing that up to conform to that shape and to the following guidelines:

1. The first, and most important, maxim of article-writing to keep in mind is: *one theme, one article*. This is why it is necessary to
    ● decide beforehand what that theme, or subject, is and
    ● give your article a working title. It doesn't matter, at this stage, if you haven't thought of a compelling one but having a title of sorts *that encapsulates the theme* will help prevent your straying from it and ending up with a piece that rambles all over the place and doesn't keep to the point.
2. Next, you must decide what the *tone* of it is to be. Do you intend it to be humorous, to bring a smile to your readers' lips? Or is it about a particularly frightening or shocking incident in your life, perhaps a warning to others not to make the same mistake? Whatever the tone, it must remain constant throughout. If it changes, the reader is likely to become irritated. If, from the opening, he believes he's meant to laugh and then, halfway through, it suddenly turns serious or even sad, he will be 'thrown' by the change of mood and, understandably, will be somewhat annoyed. (It's rather like buying a box of chocolates, believing them to be all soft-centres and discovering, part way through, that it contains some

hard-centres. You trusted the label on the box, and you are definitely not pleased.) In other words, the reader expects a signpost, at the beginning, to prepare him for the tone or mood of the piece he is about to read. (This is true of other kinds of writing, also. If, for example, we buy a horror novel, we expect to be frightened and made to shudder, not to have a laugh a minute.)

A piece intended to be funny should aim for laughs. One describing a poignant episode should aim to bring a lump to the reader's throat or a tear to the eye.

3. Next, exactly as you did when you started to plan your book, you need to brainstorm for anything that could conceivably be relevant to that particular theme or subject. Write these down, either on a large sheet of paper or on separate pieces or use the lateral-thinking method, putting the subject in the centre of the page and extending spokes outwards from it. You will want to include:
   * any incidents that illustrate your theme;
   * relevant anecdotes: these can be any related to you by someone else;
   * quotes or sayings;
   * any pertinent facts.

4. Now go through them, discarding any which, on reflection, don't seem to entirely fit, then place those remaining into a logical sequence. You are now ready to start the actual writing.

5. Above the apex of the diamond-shape, in large letters, write your title. If you can't come up with a really good one, at this stage don't worry – use a working title, for the moment.

6. Under the apex, will come your opening sentence. It must 'hook' your reader and persuade him to read on. If he is not *instantly* drawn into your piece, the chances are he will turn to another with greater appeal. It must let the reader know what the article is about and what its tone is. You cannot spend too much time on getting your

opening right because it may be all that stands between you and losing your potential reader.

The following illustrate some of the most effective openings for articles

A The statement of fact   This is designed to give the reader some information. For example:

(i)   Grandmother Johnson was a woman tiny in stature but, in character, she was a giant.

(ii)   I've visited many exotic places in the world in the years since then, but my first-ever holiday by the sea remains in my memory as the biggest adventure of my life.

(iii)   It's now nearly fifty years since that first day at school but the memory of it haunts me still.

B The question   This is particularly useful for an 'opinion' piece, especially if it is on a controversial subject. For example: Do you think children should be allowed to choose what they want to watch on TV?

C A line of dialogue   For example: 'There's no way I'm going with you!' Jennifer had yelled at me, that morning.

Each of these methods of opening an article is calculated to draw the reader into the next part of it: to want to know more. Each gives a clue as to what the rest of it will be about. Example A (i) will be about Grandmother Johnson, who was clearly an influence in the author's life; (ii) will describe the author's first holiday at the seaside and (iii) the author's first day at school which must have been either traumatic or in some way affected the rest of his or her life.

In B, the subject under discussion is obviously children's TV viewing, though we will need to read further to find out the author's opinion. Maybe he or she believes children should have free access to what they watch. If we are parents, ourselves, we may well have strong views on this and there will be a compulsion to see if the author's and ours coincide or if we will disagree violently. Either way, we want to know. Equally, I think, someone making a vehement statement cannot fail to make most of us curious about *why*. We will then have to carry on to the next sentence or two for us to be completely 'hooked'. This could be something as simple as:

I remember how my heart sank, listening to my sixteen-year-old daughter and knowing that this was one time when I could not, dare not, give in. We were emigrating to Australia in two weeks' time and she was definitely coming with us.

A reminder, here, to keep to *one theme throughout the article*. If you are describing Grandmother Johnson and her effect upon you, you must not wander off from that to relating an incident involving your grandfather or your brothers and sisters *unless it was entirely relevant*. Nor will there be time and space to cover all of her life. You want to make the point that, although tiny in build, she was full of courage and determination and that, in the future, whenever you felt daunted by what lay ahead, you recalled your grandmother and how she coped with fortitude with every vicissitude in her path – and it helped get you through those difficulties.

Once you have a title (even if only a working one) which indicates the theme or subject, and an arresting opening, you must proceed to develop:

7. The body of the article, expanding outwards to the sides of the diamond-shape as you relate relevant anecdotes, incidents, quotations, sayings, and so on, in the order in which you have arranged them. Keep in mind the following:

   ● Include some dialogue to help you *show* what happened rather than tell it, thus bringing the scene to life for your reader, making it more colourful, entertaining and illuminating.

- Include any salient *facts* that back up the point you are making or make it clearer to the reader. A useful method is to give them in the form of a comparison.
- Be specific: 'When in doubt, find out. If you can't find out, leave it out' is a good maxim to keep in mind.

Finally, you are ready to 'wind down' and bring the piece to:

8. A satisfying conclusion. The simplest and most effective way of achieving this is to draw together all the threads and round it off by *returning to the beginning*. To illustrate this, you might conclude the previous examples with:

(i) I will ever be grateful that my Grandmother Johnson was around throughout my formative years. For, without her shining example, I might never have learned to fight back whenever life dealt me one of its many hard blows.

(ii) Perhaps it was that week at x, all those years ago, that instilled in me my life-long love of the sea. Maybe that's why I chose the coast for my retirement and have never once regretted it.

(iii) Now, looking back after almost half a century, I can give a wry smile as I remember that small boy standing so forlorn and frightened in the midst of.a noisy, shabbily-clad throng of children. But nothing that happened throughout the following years ever seemed so terrifying to me as that first day at school.

To sum up: to write a successful article (or short section of your life story) remember the following guidelines:

- Keep to one theme or subject throughout.
- Have a good lead sentence(s) that will 'hook' your readers and tell them, immediately, what the article is

94

about and set its tone – is it serious, sad, nostalgic, humorous or plain shocking?

- Include anecdotes, incidents, quotations, sayings, vivid descriptions, indeed, anything that will help illustrate your theme and make your piece entertaining and illuminating. And include some dialogue, if at all possible and some facts.
- Return to the beginning to achieve a satisfying, aesthetically-pleasing ending.
- Take sufficient time to find an apt and eye-catching title.
- Keep your style simple with short, rather than long, sentences and paragraphs and write in the way you speak.

The following is one of my own 'country' articles (mentioned under Finding A Market) which illustrates the above guidelines:

Title Blacksmith Fred – Like Finding A Goldmine.
This encapsulates the theme of the article, giving the reader the first clue as to the subject. It is apt, likening Fred to gold which is also worked by a smith.

Lead sentence intended to 'hook' the reader, instantly, telling him what the article is about: 'Finding a good blacksmith, these days, is like finding a goldmine so, when Charlie Webber, a farmer in our village, said he wanted to go and see his blacksmith, I jumped at the chance.'

The 'body' of the article (including anecdotes, dialogue, descriptions, and so on):

We had just bought a badly-neglected pony from the market. Tommy was a skewbald, white with big gingery-·brown patches, a curly ginger forelock that dangled over his eyes and a gorgeous blond, wavy mane. But his ribs and hip bones stuck out and he walked like an old woman with corns, his feet needed attention so badly.

We go on to learn that the blacksmith's name is Fred and Charlie Webber is described:

> Fred was bending over the hind foot of a big black hunter near the open front of the forge when we arrived. Charlie said, 'I've brought this 'ere young lady to see 'ee. I've told her, 'ee'll shoe her horse.'
>
> Fred looked at Charlie and then at me, scratched the back of his head and muttered, ''Orses, 'orses, 'orses! There's two blacksmiths down with flu and the other chappie won't do 'em no more. I'm sorry, lady, but I can't take no more.'

More conversation as we try to persuade Fred to agree. At last, he asks:

> 'What's your name, then?'
> 'Smith,' I replied.
> A toothless grin spread over Fred's thin face – and I knew I'd won. 'Oh, come in me dinner hour, one day,' he said, 'and I'll sneeze 'ee in.'

Descriptions follow about my first visit to the forge with Tommy and watching Fred handle other horses as we await our turn, in the subsequent months and years.

> If you are cold, for the sun never penetrates the depths of his corrugated forge, he'd say, 'Come 'ee inside by the fire and get a warm.' And you could stand pumping the long wooden handle of the barrel-shaped bellows while Fred puts the horse-shoes into the fire, takes them out red-hot and hammers them deftly into shape on the anvil.

End the article by returning to beginning, to 'round it off'; 'Yes, Fred has taught me a great deal about horses and, to me, he is worth his weight in gold.'

Let's now consider some of the different types of articles you might like to try, based on personal experience, for which there is a definite market and which have a legitimate place in your autobiography.

Travel

Fifty years ago, travel, for most of us, was confined to the British Isles visited by road or rail. Today, globe-trotting by air is nothing exceptional, large numbers of people having been to most countries in Europe and even further. Therefore, in order to captivate your audience, it is necessary either to describe unusual methods of travel (horse-drawn, perhaps), or of days long gone which are sufficiently picturesque with nostalgic echoes so they will appeal to both older and younger generations. Or perhaps you can tell of journeys to less well-known places in far-flung corners of the world, many of which still have a romantic, magical allure. But whichever place you choose, whether you were there on holiday or for business purposes, in order to create in your reader's mind a true and colourful picture of it, we're back to selection: picking out the significant and deleting the unimportant elements.

How many of you, I wonder, have been bored almost to tears by hours spent viewing the holiday slides of friends because no attempt had been made to choose those which were of special interest, those which highlighted the delights and wonders of the country visited, and included too many of the more mudane aspects? The same applies to writing about them. You need to recreate on paper the sights and sounds, the colours, smells, the people, their dress, customs, foods and so on. And you need to carefully choose the words you use to do so, avoiding bland generalisations such as 'magnificent, excellent, imposing, striking, beautiful, breathtaking', searching, instead, for words that will conjure up for the reader those scenes you, yourself, remember so vividly.

Remember the importance of *emotion*, of putting across how you felt at the particular time you are describing. I clearly remember my own feelings when, after years of yearning and waiting, I finally beheld the pyramids of ancient Egypt; how I caught my breath at my first view of them, rearing up, majestically, into an azure sky beneath a searing hot sun, eternal monuments both to man's greatness and to his cruelty when we remember the long years in which many thousands of slaves toiled to build them. I remember, too, the sense of intrusion as the coaches disgorged their hordes of sightseers, to be immediately besieged by the dark-eyed, olive-skinned touts, turbanned and clad in long white or blue galabeyahs, intent upon persuading us to clamber up on to their gaudily ornamented camels. But, as we lumbered ungainly up to the foot of the Great Pyramid of Cheops, rising out of the desert at Giza, I reflected that it was only the outward trappings that had changed and nothing could really detract from the achievement of the ancient Egyptians of nearly five thousand years ago.

But, despite the undoubted awe-inspiring magnificence of the pyramids and the Sphinx, they are a part of the world's history and we should remember that people are interested in people, so what of the present-day Egyptian? Has life, for him, changed all that much, down the centuries? Your reader will want to know, to see him or her against the backcloth of those famous antiquities.

Although I have often told friends about that holiday of a lifetime, I have never, until now, attempted to record some of the tiny but heart-warming experiences when I encountered the ordinary man in the street. Wandering, alone, through the famous Khan El-Khalili bazaar in the bustling heart of Cairo, one burning hot day in May, I drank in the sounds of Arabic voices, arguing, bartering, chattering. I tried not to stare at the men, tranquilly smoking hubble-bubble water pipes outside the cafés. I gazed into the windows in the Street of Gold, filled with glistening jewellery – bracelets, necklaces and cartouches inscribed with hieroglyphics. I resisted the temptation to buy brassware but succumbed to purchasing two tiny pieces of perfectly matched amber to have made into earrings on my return home. Strolling through the crowded streets, I was suddenly accosted by a small boy, perhaps seven years of age, wearing the ubiquitous nightgown-like galabeyah 'Baksheesh,' he demanded, holding out his hand. 'Baksheesh.'

I shook my head and said, sternly, 'La!' (which means 'No') and walked on. Moments later, he ran after me, head hanging, sheepishly, his face flushed with embarrassment. 'Sorry', he murmured in English and I knew, instantly, his importuning had been noticed by one of the men, nearby, and he had been told to apologise.

Self-help

This is where you relate how you overcame a specific personal problem which you hope will help others cope with the same difficulty.

Character Sketch

These can sometimes be found in both magazines and regional newspapers but they need to be slanted to a definite market. For example, one student wrote about a Lancashire man who had never missed a Bolton Wanderers football match in fifty years and sold it to a Lancashire-based magazine.

Dramatic Incidents

These appeal to the average reader's liking to be vicariously shocked and horrified. There is an example in Section 6 entitled Incident in Iran.

Humorous Incidents

Humour is at a premium everywhere and, if you can write a truly funny personal experience, you should have no difficulty in finding a market.

99

Unusual Incident

This could, perhaps, be about something you believe to be supernatural or a strange coincidence that could not be explained.

Viewpoint

Occasionally, readers' viewpoints are specifically asked for and this is one of the few times when it is all right to express your personal opinion about something. Controversial articles can sometimes find a market in a newspaper because they stir up reader reaction.

FINDING A MARKET

Let's now take a look at where it might be possible to sell a short, complete piece of autobiographical writing as an article. Personal experiences are popular with a wide range of magazines, including those termed 'women's magazines', while national, as well as regional, newspapers take the occasional one, often having a definite slot for these.

It is essential to study a particular publication *before* submitting material to the editor. And even looking through one of the books that list current markets and their requirements (see Section 7) is no substitute for you, yourself, reading and analysing several recent issues of the one you are aiming at. In any case, useful as they undoubtedly are, magazine editors and/or policies may have changed between such books being compiled and reaching publication, so that some of their information might well be out of date.

I can hear some of you saying that it's expensive having to buy copies of different magazines and newspapers just to study them. Yes, that is true. But most households take one or two publications regularly so ask your family, friends and neighbours to let you have a look at some of theirs. Browse along the magazine racks in some of the larger newsagents: you may find one or two you hadn't seen or heard of before which might be suitable outlets. If some of their articles are obviously of the personal experience variety, it will probably be worth buying a copy to study in detail at home. And don't forget most doctors' and dentists' waiting rooms and hairdressers' salons usually provide a selection to while away the waiting time so take advantage of them, the next occasion you're there.

Because new magazines spring up and others, sadly, disappear, from time to time, it is difficult to mention specific markets. However, you might consider the following types as possible outlets for your work.

'Countryside/Green' magazines   These tend to carry character sketches, nostalgic pieces and anything to do with ancient traditions and customs pertaining to country living.

Regional magazines   These tend to be monthly and contain features of interest to people living in a specific region, though you don't necessarily have to reside in the area to submit material. If, for instance, your Great-Uncle Joseph lived all his life in the same town and was a faithful follower of the local football/cricket/sports club for fifty years, it is quite possible the editor would jump at a profile of him because many of his readers would find it of interest.

Religious magazines   Here, the slant must obviously be towards Christian living and values. If you have an unusual, uplifting or spiritually-moving incident to relate or, say, had an aunt who founded a local church group, x years ago, perhaps against great odds, that might appeal to the editor.

Specialist magazines   It is worth keeping an eye open for slots in magazines covering a specific subject – health, hobbies or retirement, for instance. Suppose you had overcome a certain condition through a particular diet, an account of that might well prove acceptable to the editor. And a writer friend of mine sold an article to one of the 'retirement' magazines on her experiences fleeing from the path of the advancing German army, tying it in with the fiftieth anniversary of the start of the last war, thus giving it a topical slant.

Women's magazines   There is such a vast range of these that you need to keep looking out for specific 'personal experience' slots. Some I have seen include a long-running series of 'When I was a Child' (see example in Section 6), and topics such as 'It Happened to Me'; 'A Heart-Warming Experience'; 'My Most Romantic Moment'. Often, these pieces are very well paid.

National and regional newspapers   Some national papers have occasional slots for personal experience articles. Regional newspaper editors are often happy to take occasional pieces, perhaps to fill in on days when there is a shortage of news or to add a lighter touch if it is humorous in tone. After my family moved from the city to live in the country I had many short, light-hearted pieces in our local 'rag'.

Finally, it is not impossible to create your own particular slot by being aware of current trends and of finding a gap in the market. Many years ago, I did just that, at a time when the 'green' movement and the idea of 'getting back to nature' were growing in popularity. I suggested to a women's magazine that they might like a regular series of light countryside pieces: the result was my own monthly spot which ran for nearly two years.

All of these markets are available to the discerning writer of autobiography, provided you do your market research, first, and make sure you send the right material of the right length to the right market.

Analysing the Market

1. Beg, borrow or buy several recent issues of whichever publication(s) you feel might be suitable for the kind of piece you want to write or have already written.
2. Read carefully to find out the readership at which is is aimed: mainly female, male and female, their age/socio-economic group, likely careers and leisure activities, broad interests and so on. A good indication of these is always provided by the advertisements, so pay particular attention to these.
3. Try to discover which articles are staff-written (this should become obvious after studying the by-lines in several issues) and which seem to be by freelance contributors.
4. What type (humorous, nostalgic, serious, and so on) and number of personal experiences are used regularly?
5. What is the average length used? Count the number of words to find out. It is no use submitting an article of 2000 words if nothing longer than 1000 appears to be ever printed.
6. Study titles (though editors often change them, it is still important to choose an eye-catching one, yourself)' and take a close look at opening sentences.

If you tackle writing your short personal experience pieces in this professional way, you will stand a good chance of selling some of them, also.

◇

Taking it further

AUTOBIOGRAPHICAL NOVELS

You may wish to write, not a true autobiography, but rather a novel based on your life. Also, it is quite possible that, after working on your life story, you become so fascinated by the whole process that you decide to continue after that is finished, as did a student of mine, some years ago, going on to complete a novel.

Whilst it is probably true to say that most fiction has germinated from some experience of the author, none the less, the autobiographical novel is what might be called, in gardening terms, a hybrid. It is an amalgam of fact and fiction – or faction, to use a newly-coined expression. But hybrid though it might be, its classification is very definitely a novel. Therefore, a few timely words of warning.

Bearing in mind Henry James's dictum that life is all inclusion and confusion and art is all discrimination and selection, attempting to put down the events of your life *exactly as they happened* is a sure-fire way of killing your novel (or short story, for that matter) stone dead before you even begin.

It is often said that first novels are mainly autobiographical. This may well be true, because a wise maxim is 'write about what you know' until you are skilled and experienced. And, if there is one thing we all know more about than anything else, it is our own lives. But in a work of fiction, however much real life is drawn upon within its pages, the truth has to manipulated and *structured*.

Somerset Maugham knew what it was like to suffer the agonies of a dreadful stammer and to lose a beloved mother when he was a child. However, in writing what he, himself, termed an autobiographical novel (*Of Human Bondage*), being a consummate craftsman, he gave his main character, Philip, the handicap of a club foot, not a stammer. He then devised a plot which, though drawing upon *emotions* he had undoubtedly experienced, himself, was basically fiction.

Emotion, as we have already seen, is a key ingredient in successful writing of all kinds and never more so than in fiction. And, whilst our lives may have differed considerably from others people's, we will each have known the full gamut of emotions and thus can imbue our characters with these. For instance, there can be few who do not know what it is to love deeply, to feel jealousy, envy, anger, hate (or a dislike so intense that it is close to hate), grief, tenderness and so on.

You will need to employ all the various fictional techniques discussed in this book when writing any kind of novel. The major difference between the latter and a true autobiography lies in its construction. (Those interested in learning more about fiction writing, in general, might find *The Fiction Writers' Handbook* useful: see Section 7.)

Never forget that a novel, however close it stays to events that have actually happened, is essentially a work of fiction. Its starting point, therefore, must always be at, or close to, *a point of change*, in the main character's life. It is from that point of change, that initial moment of crisis, that the tension of the story is set up. The story then begins to rise in a series of peaks, rather like the folds of a mountain, dropping down into troughs as minor problems are solved and rising again as others are introduced, but always leading inexorably upwards until the summit, the climax, is reached and thence to the resolution and the story's end.

But these tensions, these problems, these crisis points are all artificially created by you, the writer, as a means of persuading the reader to keep on turning the pages until the end. This is part and parcel of the craftsmanship of writing.

Nancy Hale, discussing autobiograhical fiction in her excellent book, *The Realities of Fiction*, says that: 'Phantasy may in the end produce a result more closely resembling the atmosphere of truth than grim adherence to, say, chronology will.' She goes on to suggest that this particular kind of fiction is nothing if not an art; that it attempts to render a truth, not to the past as it once, possibly, existed but to the past as it exists in relation to the present and the future; that this kind of truth is an artistic and not a literal one.

Perhaps the main advantage of autobiographical fiction is that it frees the writer from any obligation to stick to the truth, even if that truth is only the one that he, himself, perceives. It may also be that a budding writer (of any age), seeking a springboard from which to launch himself into the previously untested waters of fiction, needs to have a solid base from which to dive and using his own life as that base will give him that necessary feeling of security.

In the following extract from *An Australian Childhood*, a novel largely based on the writer's own childhood, note how the feeling of intense heat is created by the careful choice of words and phrases like: 'the sky seemed clamped on like a hot, blue lid'; 'a great oven of ochre clay and dying vegetation'; 'the first rays felt like little burning fingers'; 'the mad dance of heatwaves into an implacable sky', and so on.

The writing is intensely visual, aided by the use of fresh and appropriate similes: 'it caught on like a bushfire'; 'he loped like a kangaroo'; 'they scattered like a flock of startled budgerigars'. .

The painfully sad hopelessness of Billy Barrett comes across as we watch him gazing, unmoving, out of the window; see an elbow protecting his ear and his eyes seeking escape. The character is clearly drawn from life, even if Billy Barrett was not his real name.

Waiting for the Rain by Dianne Morris

On that first day of the seventh grade, the sky clamped on like a hot, blue lid. We all sweated over our new exercise books but none more uncomfortably than the new boy, Billy Barrett. From time to time, he would shake his head from side to side as if to activate whatever might be inside it. It was also the action of someone used to dealing with a constant settling of flies around his face. Eventually, his eyes drifted upwards to the tops of the kurrajong trees and telegraph poles outside. With his pencil clutched in one hand, he stayed in that position for at least half an hour without moving.

It was January, and the first day of a new school year, when we children of the west must relinquish the worship of the town swimming-pool and imprison our bodies, once again, in school uniform and shoes. But not Billy Barrett. His grease-stained shorts, snarled-up hair and bare feet alone would have set him apart from the rest of us. But what claimed my attention most was the expression in his eyes. It reminded me of a picture I'd seen of one of the great apes behind bars.

And yet we were all trapped, not only in our desks but in a great oven of ochre clay and dying vegetation. Each morning, the sun rose in a triumphant blaze of hard gold. Even the first rays felt like little burning fingers to the skin and, by midday, the tin roofs of the town would be gleaming white-hot, and the only movement to be seen would be the mad dance of heatwaves into an implacable sky. Each evening, the sun celebrated its dominion in awesome displays of purple and orange and, with a last fierce wink, promised to return. It had not rained one drop for eighteen months.

In a town such as ours, travellers passing through were treated politely, but a newcomer in its midst aroused deep suspicion and curiosity. So it had to happen, sooner or later, that someone would make the first move towards

107

solving the mystery of Billy Barrett. In this case, it was the class smart-alecs, Gordon O'Shea and Peter Kenney, who started poking him with rulers and sniggering. This was a fairly standard overture. The newcomer could acquit himself well by either retaliating or grinning and putting up with it. The worst type damned themselves by telling the teacher. But Billy did none of these things. Roused from his contemplation of the tree-tops, he turned round slowly and gaped at his tormentors until they uneasily put away their rulers, pulling faces at each other to suggest that Billy had a screw loose, somewhere. That was when Mr Brown looked up and saw them.

His eyes followed the pointing fingers to see Billy with his head ducked down on to the desk and an elbow stuck up to protect his ear. 'Stay in ten minutes after the bell, the lot of you,' he roared.

Ignoring the mutters of indignation, he walked over to Billy and squatted beside him. 'How's it going?' he asked gently. Billy disengaged his head and looked blank. Mr Brown wrote something on the page then, finally, patted him on the head and sent him out for morning break.

A knot of girls gathered round the water-taps as I splashed my burning face and I lingered to hear what they were saying. It was about Billy Barrett and the speaker was the police sergeant's daughter.

'He's got no mum so his dad takes him droving, but he's out of work, now. There's no droving because of the drought, see. Anyway, Dad went out to their camp at the two-mile, yesterday. He said if he didn't see that kid here, today, he'd have him taken away to a home. They'd make him go to school there. Dad said they live like blacks, no dunny or anything.'

There was a murmur of disgust as all eyes moved towards Billy, slouching in the corner by the rubbish bins. He was examining a brown-paper packet.

'Heh, that's me sandwiches I just threw out,' said one of the girls, indignantly.

I could sense anger moving through the ranks like a hot breeze stirring the gum-leaves.

'I'll show him,' said someone else. She marched over, head in the air and sailed past him, holding her nose and brushing away imaginary flies. Eventually, it caught on like a bushfire until half the school was doing the same. Billy hesitated while his eyes sought an escape. Then he loped like a kangaroo out on to the burning flat of the playground while his tormentors scattered at the clanging of the bell, like a flock of startled budgerigars, up the flights of wooden stairs and into their respective classrooms.

I lingered on the high veranda to watch him, under the pretence of having a stuck lock on my new schoolbag. Heatwaves began to break up his outline before my very eyes as he stood motionless, his face turned to the sky, and one hand shading his eyes. His head moved slowly from one end of the horizon to the other with agonising thoroughness. I felt a secret thrill of understanding. Now I recognised why he had looked up, not down, out of the windows. He was looking for signs, signs of rain. But the fierce unbroken blue seemed to mock his bowed form as he climbed the stairs back to the classroom.

© Dianne Morris

WRITING A FAMILY HISTORY

'To forget one's ancestors is to be a brook without a source, a tree without a root.'
Old Chinese proverb

Some of you may feel you would like, at some stage, to go on to write up your family history, or you may wish to include a part of it in your autobiography.

Tackling a family history is likely to involve you in lengthy research, depending on how far you wish to go and how much time you are prepared to devote to it. One student worked on hers for nearly three years, with great excitement tracing previously unknown members in far-flung countries and uncovering at least one 'skeleton in the cupboard'. The result was a small, privately and inexpensively published book which not only gave tremendous pleasure to herself and her immediate family but allowed her to recoup much of the cost of printing by selling copies to most of her distant relatives, too. Relations abroad were fascinated to learn more about their English ancestors from the text, a family tree and facsimiles of their marriage, birth and death certificates and to see what they looked like from the various reproduced photographs.

But, even if you don't want to undertake as big a task as that, once you've embarked on producing your own life story, it would be foolish to miss an opportunity of talking to any of the remaining older generation, gleaning from them any snippets of information that you might be able to include. Such reminiscences could prove invaluable if, later on, you did decide to extend your own story to that of your entire family. In any case, it would probably help flesh out half-forgotten parts of your childhood. Thus it makes sense to persuade surviving elderly relatives to talk about the past, to tell you what it was like when they were growing up, earlier this century, before it is too late. Beg them to let you. see any old photographs or items of memorabilia they have tucked away, somewhere. Who knows what interesting anecdotes and bits of your family's past might come to light?

If you have to make a journey in order to 'interview' an ageing relative, you would find it useful to have a list of questions ready prepared. If you contact them by post, enclosing a simple questionnaire asking for the information you require should ensure a quick reply. And enclosing a stamped, self-addressed envelope would be a courtesy, also. For example, if you are trying to trace ancestors on your father's side, you could include the following questions:

- Father's name
- Date of birth
- Place of birth
- Schools attended with dates, if possible

- Jobs/profession, including qualifications, if any, and where obtained
- Period in armed forces – when and where, if known
- Places of residence with dates, if possible
- Date and place of marriage
- Date and place of birth of children

Tracing one's family history is a pastime rapidly growing in popularity and there are specialist agencies who will undertake the necessary research, though this can prove quite expensive. There are also various national and local societies which it would be worth joining if you are seriously interested. However, for those willing to do their own research, I have listed some of the main sources of reference.

Since 1 July 1837, all births, marriages and deaths have been required by law to be registered, thus it should be possible to trace back four or even five generations. But remember you may have to check and verify spelling of names because, years ago when many were unable to read or write, someone else would write them down, frequently spelling them phonetically, accounting for the variations so often found. Dates of birth, especially, but also of marriage and death, might not have been recorded accurately, possibly deliberately but perhaps in error.

The best place to start is with living relatives, getting as much information as possible from them. After that, go to the following sources:

Family documents including wills, letters, diaries, deeds and certificates of any kind, not forgetting family Bibles which frequently contained valuable records of all kinds.

County Records Offices most archivists will help you with searching for relevant information. Microfiche should be available, recording everything in their collection which ought to include parish registers (below).

Public records for England and Wales are kept at St Catherine's House, 10 Kingsway, London WC2B 6JP, where you personally inspect their index volumes though not the actual registers.

Parish Registers since 1538, parish registers have recorded baptisms, marriages and burials, some of which may not have been deposited at the local County Records Office so it is worth checking these.

The International Genealogical Index (IGI) compiled and kept by the Church of Latter Day Saints (Mormon Church), is on microfiche at the London Regional Genealogical Library (Mormon Branch Library), 64/68 Exhibition Road, South Kensington, London SW7 2PA. This can be a useful starting point for researching family history. A small fee is charged for each film examined.

Boyd's Marriage Index lists marriages in England between 1538 and 1837. Contact The Society of Genealogists, 14 Charterhouse Buildings, Goswell Road, London EC1M 7BA for further information.

Divorce Registry records of all divorces since 1852 are held at Somerset House, Strand, London WC2R 1LP.

Census Returns 19th-century returns are held on microfilm in the Census Room of the Public Record Office in Portugal Street, London (further information from the Public Record Office, Chancery Lane, London WC2A 1LR). From 1851, more in-depth information is given as to age, place of birth, and so on.

British Library Newspaper Library, Colindale Avenue, London NW9 5HE has copies of all British newspapers, as well as some from other countries world-wide, and is open every day except Sunday with free access. You may wish to check

announcements or read reports of relevant events or incidents.

Family Search Programme   By the time this book is published,
you may be able to undertake much of your research into
tracing your ancestors by going no further than your local
public library. The programme, recently launched by Dynix
Library Systems, will include the International Genealogical
Index (details of 147 million people, mostly dating from 1500
to 1875), plus an Ancestral File. It will be possible to search
this Index by name and country, while the Ancestral File will
enable you to look backwards and forwards along family
lines. For further details, see Section 7.

Family Tree Magazine   is a monthly periodical devoted to
this subject (see Section 7).

A word of warning: although the keeping of parish registers
became a legal requirement in 1538, in practice, this didn't
always happen. Also, if you are going back several centuries,
you will find gaps throughout the Civil War and
Commonwealth period of 1645 – 60.

There are various useful publications readily available for
those interested in pursuing this further, a few of which are
listed in Section 7.

Some of you may find yourselves being side-tracked from
your own life story when you start introducing other, long-
departed members of the family. You may begin to wonder
where your mother's unusual maiden name originated, for
instance, and that is enough to set you off. In fact, writing
your personal life-story could be just the beginning of a
whole new project that will keep you occupied and engrossed
for years to come.

TALES TO TELL

Even if you don't want to write your own life story, at this stage, or are perhaps a little afraid of doing so, you could play your part in preserving for posterity some small segment of our heritage by recording, before it is too late, the lives of others.

In the midst of writing this book, I happened to start talking to an assistant in my local secondhand bookshop. 'Oh,' she said, 'I've often wished I'd recorded some of the stories our elderly neighbour used to tell about life in this village when he was a boy.' He'd died, she told me, at the age of ninety and had loved nothing better than to regale anyone who would listen with what it had been like for humble folk like himself in those far-off days. It occurred to me, then, that there was a place in this book for advocating the preservation, in any form whatever, of some of the life stories of others. There must be many like that old man who have fascinating tales to tell about social mores, customs, traditions long gone, about ways of life in towns and villages and countryside throughout the land that have vanished into the mists of time. And, unless some of us take it upon ourselves to record them, they will be lost forever for future generations.

So, if you don't yet feel up to digging into your own personal history, why not do some limbering-up exercises by putting down on paper the stories of others? All you really need for this is their willingness to chat about the past and a simple tape-recording machine. Most modern radio/cassette players have a built-in tape-recorder which is perfectly adequate for this purpose.

It's probably best to get people talking naturally before switching it on, otherwise they might become inhibited and sound stilted. And have a list of questions ready in case they begin to dry up. If they're in the least gregarious and sociable, however, you're not likely to need them. And it doesn't matter *how* they relate their stories, all jumbled up

114

together with one incident mixed up with another as they change tack in the middle. Once they've finished, it will be your job to unravel it and put it into some sort of order on paper.

Here are a few of the questions you could have prepared in case they are needed or which you could follow up with if you feel you need more detail:

- What was it like when you first came to live in X?
- How did you travel to the nearest town or city?
- How old were you when you went to school/left school?
- What was your first job?
- Did you spend the rest of your working life in the same one?
- What is your earliest memory?
- How did you meet your wife/husband?
- What did you do in the war?
- How have you spent your retirement?
- Have you any advice to the young people of today?

One big advantage of making a tape-recording of someone speaking is that, when you come to transpose it on to the page, you have their actual words and speech-patterns to draw on. Obviously, you need to edit the dialogue, otherwise it is likely to be unreadable with its 'ums' and 'ers' and interjections, but this is where your skill as a budding writer will come in. Whilst sticking as closely as possible to the account you're hearing, you can weave the dialogue into the narrative as seems appropriate, adding bits of description to give the piece colour, and so on.

Remember that if you, yourself, want to write all or part of your life story but, because of arthritis or other disability, are physically unable to put pen to paper, you can record it in the same way.

❧

Practical issues

REVISION

Few, if any, writers never need to revise their work. Some do it as they proceed but most will get their first draft down on paper without worrying too much about *how* it's written, and then, when it's finished, go over it, pruning, polishing and tightening it, generally editing until it is as near perfect as they can make it. (Catherine Cookson's autobiography *Our Kate* went through eight drafts before it achieved publication.) It is advisable to check the following:

- That you haven't been over-lavish with adjectives and adverbs. If you find you have, cut out some of the former and, where possible, exchange the latter for stronger verbs.
- That you haven't used clichés or hackneyed phrases but have found fresh images and ways of describing things.
- That you haven't constantly used the same word in the same piece. This can be very irritating to the reader and it only needs a little more thought to re-word or, very often, it can be omitted without affecting the sense. A thesaurus is useful for finding alternative words.
- That your spelling and grammar are impeccable. If in doubt, consult a dictionary and/or grammar book or ask

someone whose knowledge of English you trust to read it through for you.

- That you haven't included over-long, unwieldy sentences or paragraphs. If you have, break them up. For example, sentences can easily be divided by starting a new one using a conjunction: '*But* my sister wouldn't listen'; or: '*And* so we left the old house early the next morning'. (That old grammatical rule of never starting a sentence with a conjunction or ending with a preposition no longer applies. In fact, it is not only acceptable but is often preferable, today, largely because of the influence of modern journalism.)

- That you've started your book or each separate piece at the right place so that your reader's attention is grabbed *immediately*.

An advantage of belonging to a writer's group of any kind is the opportunity to read out parts of your book, thus benefiting from the feedback from other members. If, however, you are working in isolation and do not have that advantage, be wary of allowing family or friends to read and comment on it. For one thing, they may not be sufficiently objective: they may either be too lavish with praise or go to the other extreme and be too critical so far as style, at least, is concerned.

Long before you have reached the point of revision, however, you will have decided if your book is intended as a family record only or if you intend aiming for a wider readership. Having planned its structure, put into effect the various fictional techniques described earlier in order to add colour and clarity to your story, if you wish to interest a publisher in it, you will need to become your own critic. You will need to prune and polish, check grammar and spelling, take another look at your style: in fact, make your book as near perfect as you possibly can before submitting it to the coldly detached eye of a publisher.

You will probably need to re-write your first few pages to

ensure you will capture your reader's (and potential editor's) attention instantly. This is where it will pay dividends to take another close look at how successful autobiographies begin, then ask yourself: Could I possibly improve my opening? Would starting with a line of dialogue, maybe, make mine more eye-catching? Or should I have begun with a more startling or dramatic 'hook'? But whether you are writing short personal experience pieces as separate articles or a complete book, revision is an essential part of the process. ·

Here is a short piece produced by one of my students. It was her first attempt at an article and she has kindly given permission for her first draft to be reproduced, together with the final version which was subsequently submitted to the editor of a specialist (religious) magazine.

Christmas in Bethlehem/The Lemon Tree by Anne Matthews (*first draft*).

Vida and Giles, my sister and brother-in-law, both doctors from Dartmouth in Devon, arrived here on Christmas Eve 1981. They were determined to have Christmas in Bethlehem.

I was living there in a simple rented flat belonging to Im and Abu Haddah who, with their large family, goats and chickens, occupied the ground floor. The house had been built without a plan or planning permission on a stony olive grove slope in the Judaean hills. There was a lemon tree standing on its own on the patio. The breathtaking panorama around it included the Shepherds' Fields, Dead Sea, Mountains of Moab and was dominated by the silhouette of Bethlehem, itself.

There was no time to waste. We had to get to Rachel's Tomb, on the outskirts of the city, to be able to join in the Latin Patriarch's solemn procession from Jerusalem for the annual celebration of Mass at midnight in St Catherine's Catholic church in Manger Square beside the huge Greek Orthodox basilica, partly built over the traditional site of Jesus' birth.

solving the mystery of Billy Barrett. In this case, it was the
the western Christians, then by the Greek and Armenian
Orthodox churches.

Crowds from all over the western world made the
approach road difficult with the strictest of Israel's security
in full operation. Armed soldiers and police with revolvers
every few yards, no matter which way we turned. At three
different points, we were checked, searched and frisked
before being allowed into Manger Square and the church,
even though we had official tickets to take part in the
singing and dancing before High Mass began, knowing the
town and Mr Freis, the Mayor.

We were able to find our way to the roof of the newly-
built Municipality in the square where we assured good-
natured Jewish soldiers patrolling on the rooftop that we
were not terrorists but innocent British tourists.

It was intensely cold with a clear sky and stars so bright
that it seemed any one of them could have led the wise men
from the East to the stable where the Prince of Peace was
born. Giles took photographs in an effort to capture something of the magic reality of the night and bring something of
it back home with him. We felt ourselves charged with a life
beyond our own, a life arising from the power of Christ.

It was then time to make our way to St Catherine's for the
midnight celebration. The tickets purchased some weeks
before allowed us to enter after waiting in a long queue for a
good hour. We didn't mind; nobody minded. We were all
part of one big family. The mystery of God becoming
human and allowing himself to be born as a helpless infant
was foremost in our hearts, telling us to become part of His
personal mystery, leaving ideas and words behind. Now we
were about to offer the Sacrifice of Love and Thanksgiving
in return for this great gift of Faith.

The Israeli Mayor of Jerusalem, Teddy Kollek, was
seated with Christian dignitaries in the front row. The
organ played as the Patriarch entered in the splendour of
his hand-embroidered vestments. A tremor went through

those of us who see ourselves as part of a church today, opting for the poor and abhorring any hint of triumphalism. But the strong smell of incense reminded us of where we were and the poverty of those living around about.

We returned to the flat about 2 a.m., cold and tired but with hearts full of gratitude and a feeling of peace. We picked a few lemons from the tree on the patio and made a much-needed hot drink before retiring to bed with our thoughts of those at home who were not lucky enough to be with us that memorable Christmas evening in Bethlehem.

Next comes the final, polished version.

Unto Us A Child is Born/The Lemon Tree by Anne Matthews

In December 1981, I was living in Bethlehem in a simple, rented flat belonging to a Palestinian couple, Im and Abu Haddah, who, together with their family, their goats and chickens, occupied the ground floor.

The house, built with neither plan nor planning permission, stood on the stony slope of an olive grove in the Judaean hills. A single lemon tree stood on its tiny patio from which the sweeping panorama included the Shepherd's Fields, the Dead Sea and the Mountains of Moab and which was dominated by the impressive silhouette of Bethlehem itself.

On 24 December, my sister, Vida, and her husband, Giles (who had arrived from England to spend Christmas in Bethlehem), and I hastened to reach Rachel's Tomb on the outskirts of the city to join in the Latin Patriarch's solemn procession. This commenced in Jerusalem, four miles away, and ended in Manger Square at St Catherine's Church (beside the huge Greek Orthodox basilica, partly built over the traditional site of Jesus' birth), with the annual celebration of midnight Mass.

Here, in Manger Square, Christmas Day is celebrated three times, first by the western Christians on 25

December, then by the Greek Orthodox Church on 6 January and, two weeks later, by the Armenians.

People from all over the western world thronged the approach road, making our passage difficult, especially with the strictest of Israel's security in full operation: armed soldiers and police with revolvers, every few yards, no matter which way we turned. At three different points, we were stopped, searched and frisked before being allowed into Manger Square and the church, even though we had official tickets (courtesy of Mr Freis, the Mayor of Bethlehem) enabling us to take part in the traditional singing and dancing before High Mass began.

Eventually, we found our way to the roof of the newly-built Municipality in the Square, where we assured the good-natured Jewish soldiers patrolling on the rooftop that we were not terrorists but merely innocent British tourists.

It was intensely cold with a clear sky and stars so bright that it seemed any one of them could have led the wise men from the East to the stable where, two thousand years ago, the Prince of Peace was born. Giles busily took photographs to capture something of the magic of that night and take it back home with them. Each of us, I believe, felt charged with a life beyond our own, a life arising from the power of Christ.

Then it was time to make our way to St Catherine's for the midnight celebration. Tickets purchased some weeks before allowed us to enter, though not before waiting in a long queue for a good hour. We didn't mind, though. Nobody minded. We were all part of one big family. The mystery of God becoming human, allowing himself to be born as a helpless infant, was foremost in our hearts, urging us to become part of His personal mystery, leaving mere words behind. Now, we were about to offer the sacrifice of love and thanksgiving in return for this great gift of Faith.

The Israeli Mayor of Jerusalem, Teddy Kollek, was seated with the Christian dignitaries in the front row. The organ thundered as the Patriarch entered, magnificent in the splendour of his richly-embroidered vestments. A tremor ran through me, abhorring any hint of triumphalism, but the strong smell of incense soon reminded me of where we were and of the poverty of those living all around.

It was two in the morning by the time we returned to my flat, cold and tired but with hearts filled with gratitude and a wonderful sense of peace. We paused to pick a few lemons from the tree on the patio to make a welcome hot drink before retiring to bed, our thoughts with those at home not lucky enough to be with us on that memorable Christmas Eve in Bethlehem.

The symbolism of the lemon tree in this piece adds greatly to its richness. It is symbolic of life, itself, through the birth of Christ, and of nourishment, both spiritual and physical – spiritual through the celebratory Mass and physical through its fruit providing a warming drink, afterwards. Personally, I prefer the title 'The Lemon Tree' which is colourful, apt and, I think, intriguing.

Most novelists accept as a matter of course the need to revise and to re-write their first chapter. By the time you have reached the end of your life story, you should be able to at least view those sections you wrote several months before with the detachment necessary for any good critic.

Working Tools

A few words of advice on the practical tools of the trade seem appropriate, especially with the advent of so much new technology in the form of electric and electronic typewriters and, of course, wordprocessors.

It is essential to submit typed work to an editor or publisher and, if you have to pay a professional typist, obviously that adds to the cost of preparing your book. If you don't possess a machine of any kind, it is worth considering buying one, especially if you think you might continue to write after you've finished this project. And even if you can't type already, age is no barrier to learning. A student of mine bought a secondhand electric typewriter, and taught herself, when she was eighty-eight, solely in order to produce her autobiography in readable form for her large family. A prolific fiction-writer acquaintance of mine bought, and taught herself to use, a wordprocessor when she was approaching her eightieth birthday.

The biggest advantage of using a wordprocessor is the ease with which corrections can be made. Thus it doesn't matter how inexperienced a typist you are because mistakes can be put right at the touch of a key without all that messy white correcting fluid or rubbers we used to need. It also speeds up the revision of your work, enables you to switch sections of it round if you feel they aren't in the right place, and produce a finished MS for submission to an editor that is flawless in appearance.

So far as cost is concerned, nowadays, it is possible to buy a simple wordprocessor comparatively cheaply, probably for little more than you would pay for an electric typewriter or even an electronic one.

A word of warning, however. PCWs (personal computer word-processors) are highly technical pieces of equipment and, while such machines hold no terrors to the younger generation (indeed, children of today are often besotted with them), to those of us not technically or mechanically-minded, they are frightening beasts which need to be tamed, at first. It took me three months to feel at home with mine and, during that time, I could cheerfully have thrown it out of the window on many occasions! Talking to writer friends, I was comforted to learn I wasn't alone in feeling like that. But I realised, too late, it would have been sensible to take some lessons on how to use it, first, rather than struggle to understand a manual written in what almost might have been a foreign language.

If you are fortunate enough to have someone able to teach you how to use it and be on hand for when problems arise, then you shouldn't have too much difficulty. Certainly, if you are prepared to cope with the initial problems of familiarising yourself with a PCW, you are not likely to regret having made the effort. Now that I have made friends with mine, I wonder how on earth I managed without it!

Raymond Carver, talking about the typist he employs: 'It may seem like a small thing, really, but it's changed my life, that woman with her word processor.'

GRAMMAR

I've included a short section on grammar because there are certain areas that frequently cause problems. Submitting a professional-looking typescript to an editor or publisher is of great importance, and that includes making sure spelling and punctuation, in particular, are correct. A few basic rules, therefore:

Punctuation   Only use dashes, exclamation marks and semi-colons *occasionally* and where appropriate. Often, a comma or full stop would be preferable or more correct. Quite apart from this, the look of many a MS has been spoiled by being thus cluttered.

Common nouns   should not have a capital letter: mother, father, parents, aunt, company, for instance, unless they are used as a title. For example: Aunt Maggie; Grandma Johnson; Sergeant Willis.

The apostrophe especially in the case of the possessive pronoun and plurals, seems to cause more difficulties than almost any other area of punctuation. It is really quite simple, if you take time to think of the meaning. See the following examples:
  that luggage is theirs;
  those books are yours;

please remove its coat;

whose bag is that;

Most confusion seems to arise between the possessive pronoun 'its' and the contraction of 'it is' – it's, the latter merely having the 'i' omitted because that's the way we usually speak. For example:

It's no use trying to bandage its paw.

In cases where plural nouns such as people and children are used to denote possession, the apostrophe comes immediately after the noun and before the 's': people's, children's, women's, men's. Straightforward plurals do not have an apostrophe: worlds; fields; typewriters; and so on. For example: world's (meaning more than one world) is *not* correct.

Spelling Certain words seem to cause problems. A few of those which should be checked on, if you know spelling is a weakness, are:

- Accept and except;
- Advice and advise; licence and license; practice and practise (in English usage the noun is spelled with a 'c', the verb with an 's').
- When a noun is turned into an adverb, usually a letter is lost, e.g. humour become humorously; skill becomes skilfully.
- A common mistake is writing 'all right' as if it were one word, 'alright': it is two.
- Similarly, 'none' should be followed by the singular and not the plural (none is and *not* none are).

Tense Watch that you don't change tenses, unintentionally. The simple past is the more normal one used to tell a story. The present tense (I am sitting, here, at my desk; I wake up and find myself wondering) can, on occasions, be very effective because it creates an immediacy. However, consider carefully before using it and, if you do, know *why* and for what

125

purpose. There is also an inherent danger of slipping into the past tense, unawares. (The use of the pluperfect, for introducing flashback, has already been explained in Section 2.)

Syntax Watch out for the kind of slip which attaches the verb to the wrong object. Geoffrey Ashe, in *The Art of Writing Made Simple*, gives this amusing example: 'If your baby does not thrive on raw milk, boil it.' Obviously, it is the milk which should be boiled but the faulty syntax suggests it could be the baby!

But don't let poor spelling or grammar inhibit you when you are getting your life story down on paper. It is at the revision stage that you need to check it carefully, either with a dictionary and grammar book or perhaps by asking someone to go through your MS to pick up any such errors that may have inadvertently crept in.

No writer should be without a good dictionary to hand and there are plenty readily available. *The Shorter Oxford English Dictionary*, although expensive, is still considered the best by many people even if it is a little old-fashioned now. Instead, you might try the latest edition of the *Concise Oxford Dictionary*, which is fine for most purposes, or any other more recently published one such as *The Cassell Concise English Dictionary*. Similarly, although *Fowler's Modern English Usage* provides still-valid information, a more up-to-date grammar book, such as *Practical English Grammar* by Thomson & Martinet (OUP), might prove of more help in areas of grammar.

TITLES

It is the title of your article or story which first attracts the reader's attention (and the editor's) and first reactions about anything, as we all know from our everyday lives, influence what we think about it, afterwards. It never ceases to amaze me that, when someone has laboured many hours over a piece of writing, polishing and pruning until it's as good as they can make it, they spend no time at all on seeking an appropriate and eye-catching title.

For a start, if you haven't bothered to come up with an intriguing as well as relevant title but have merely given it the most obvious one you could think of, an editor cannot help but be prejudiced against it, initially. If it is well enough written and the editor likes it and considers it suitable for publication, a poor title won't bring a rejection slip. But, if you're taking the writing game seriously, you need to do everything possible to persuade that editor to accept it – there is a lot of competition out there, all vying for limited word-space.

Here are some 'rules' and suggestions for finding good titles for your article or book and also for chapter headings, if you decide to use them:

1. It should encapsulate the *theme*: that is, give the reader a clue as to what it is about. If, for instance, it is about spending a memorable Christmas with your grandmother, we should know that from the title. But calling it 'A Memorable Christmas with my Grandmother' would hardly induce anyone to read further. You would need help to think up something much more captivating than that.

2. It should convey the *tone* of the piece, just as its opening will do. If serious in tone, it should have a serious-sounding title, reflecting the subject under discussion. If humorous, then one that suggests the reader can expect to be amused, be made to smile, at least. That way, he/she has a choice, to skip to one lighter in mood, for instance, if not wishing to think too deeply about something, at that particular moment.

3. It should be eye-catching, in some way, and alliteration is an excellent device to catch the reader's attention. For example, 'Sun, Sea, Sand and Sangria'. It would be

obvious, immediately, this was about a summer holiday in Spain and much more effective than merely calling it 'A Summer Holiday in Spain'.

4. A pun is another method of drawing the reader's (and editor's) eye to your piece. One in a magazine slanted at nostalgia for the countryside cleverly used both a pun and alliteration: 'Granny Get Your Gun'. It followed through with its promise of an entertaining incident about the author's courageous, strong-willed grandmother and ended with a humorous twist. Another, on the theme of Christmas with grandma, and obviously humorous in tone, was entitled: 'Cooking Granny's Goose'. And another, which made me laugh out loud in a dentist's waiting room as it related the problems of finding public toilets while towing a caravan, had the delightful title 'Looking for Loo-Loo'.

5. A single intriguing word can be very effective, too, especially for chapter headings. Paul Bailey uses these in *An Immaculate Mistake*, words such as 'Confetti', 'Guttersnipe', 'Wanderer'.

6. A simple phrase that gives a clue as to period and setting is yet another way to make you at least want to open the book's cover and start reading, as Helen Forrester's best-selling *Twopence to Cross the Mersey* demonstrated.

7. A line of poetry or a quotation from a play or book can work well, too, if it is apt. For example, one of the contributors to Section 6 has taken her title from a line in a poem by Longfellow: 'The sands of time'.

Suggestions for titles for sections of your autobiography (as well as perhaps for articles) are:

- The Saddest Day of My Life.
- A Day I'll Never Forget.
- The Reunion
- Homecoming
- If Only I'd Never . . .

Giving each section even a working title, at the beginning, will also help you focus on the subject matter and theme so that you don't stray as you're writing it. But never be tempted to submit your book (or article) without spending time getting the title right. It could make the difference between acceptance and rejection.

COPYRIGHT AND LIBEL

These two considerations, included together, shouldn't cause too much problem for most people writing their life story. However, there are one or two occasions when they might so it is as well to be aware of what is entailed in law.

Copyright

The UK copyright law says that any piece of writing (published or not) belongs to the person who wrote it until fifty years after his or her death – not fifty years after it was written or published, as is sometimes erroneously believed. In the case of, say, a letter, the actual paper on which it was written belongs to the recipient but the copyright of the *words themselves* does not – that is still retained by the writer or, after his death, by his or her estate.

If you had in your possession letters written to, perhaps, your father or grandfather and the author were still alive, or had not been dead for fifty years, it would not be prudent to include them or extracts from them without first obtaining written permission from the relevant party.

The same applies to diaries although the probability, here, is that, if you have access to them, they will have been written by a close family member and inherited by another member who would probably allow you to quote from them.

Copyright law, however, does have a 'fair dealing' clause which allows anyone to quote short extracts of a published work without permission (though due acknowledgement must be made in the text) for the 'purposes of criticism and review'. How long is a short extract, of course, is similar to asking how long is a piece of string but it is usually defined as meaning 'insubstantial'. In practice (as agreed, some years ago between The Society of Authors and the Publishers Association), it is generally accepted as not being more than 400 words from a long work such as a novel and not more than a quarter of a poem or short work.

If in doubt, it is wise to err on the safe side and check that you are not infringing anyone's copyright before reproducing and quoting from their work by requesting written permission. Depending upon the number of quotations you wish to use, this can be a lengthy process, involving writing, in the first instance, to the publishers (if there were subsequent editions such as a paperback, you should write to the original publishers) who is likely to hold such rights. If they don't, they will be able to tell you who does. If you wished also to include newspaper cuttings or photographs, the same law would apply and permission must be obtained.

Often, a way round this problem is to paraphrase so that you retain the meaning of the words without using the actual ones written.

Although there is no copyright in titles, you risk a possible lawsuit if you choose one already in use and which is closely identified with another author. This could be construed as attempting to 'pass off' your work as that of someone else for monetary gain.

There is no copyright in facts. But, if you are quoting facts obtained from a published book, you must not use its author's actual wording. The *facts* alone are yours for the taking: the words used to describe them must be your own.

Libel

In order to successfully sue for libel, it must be proved that an author has held the complainant up to 'hatred, ridicule or contempt' through making a defamatory statement. Again, err on the safe side when introducing into your book people who are still alive.

You cannot, of course, libel the dead. The main consideration here is likely to be a question of taste and a wish not to cause hurt or offence to anyone still living. This can only be a matter for personal judgement.

The Society of Authors has produced leaflets on both these topics, obtainable from them at a cost of £1 (free for members) – see Section 7.

YOU'VE FINISHED WRITING SO WHAT NOW?

You've finished the actual writing, so now what do you do, assuming you want to try to get your book in print? How do you set about finding a publisher? And what about literary agents? Wouldn't it be best to try to get one of them to handle everything from now on?

Well, for a start, don't be in too much of a hurry to send your book off. It's much wiser to put it away for a few weeks, then get it out, again, and take a fresh, detached look at it. It's surprising how often spelling or grammatical errors or clumsy-sounding phrases can be spotted after even a brief period has elapsed. Read it through again, carefully, and make any necessary corrections. Only then are you ready to submit it.

In the meantime, however, you should have sent some letters either to publishers, asking if they would be interested in seeing your book, or to one or two literary agents, enquiring if they would handle it for you. Keep your letter short and succinct but pay as much attention to how it's worded as you have to your book because on that may well depend their reaction. At this stage, what you want is someone agreeing to at least read it, thus avoiding having it end up on what is derisively known as the 'slush pile', that place in a publisher's office reserved for unsolicited manuscripts.

The main hurdle, so far as an autobiography is concerned, is persuading an editor or literary agent that yours will make such fascinating reading that it will sell to the 'man in the street'. In your letter, you should state the period it spans (your entire life or just one particularly interesting part of it) and its length. You should mention any work you've previously had published and if any parts of your book have appeared as articles in magazines or newspapers. Finally, ask if they would be willing to look at it, in which case you would be happy to submit either the entire MS or the first three chapters. It might also be advantageous to include a brief synopsis, if possible.

Having decided on this course of action, the next step is to choose some suitable publishers and/or agents. Both *The Writers' and Artists' Year Book* and *The Writer's Handbook* (see Section 7) list most of these and should mention which publishers take autobiography. However, you would be wise to carry out your own market study, checking in libraries and book shops to see which firms are publishing the kind of book you have written. Some may seem to favour the light-hearted James Herriot type while others the more serious ones.

It is wise to address your initial letter to a particular editor, personally. You can verify who would be the right one by making a phone call to the publisher's office and asking the switchboard operator. The following is an example of the sort of letter you could send,

Dear Mr/Ms . . .

I have just completed a part of my autobiography, spanning the years from my birth in 1921 to 1939 when I was called up into the army. It illustrates life in a farming community in rural Devon, during that period, describing its primitiveness, its deprivations, closeness to nature, the humour, the camaraderie, the sheer hard work experienced by everyone. I have also tried to show the difficulties and frustrations for a child growing up under those conditions, especially one longing for education but, as was the custom, then, frequently unable to attend school because of the necessity of helping with farm work.

I have had several short articles, based on my life story, published in (list publications), over the past few years, and enclose photocopies of two of these. The title of my book is '. . . . .' and it is approximately 60,000 words in length.

I should be very pleased to send you either the complete MS or the first three chapters plus synopsis, if you feel it might be suitable for your list.

I look forward to hearing from you, in due course, and enclose a stamped addressed envelope for your reply.

Yours sincerely

If you decide, first of all, to try to find a literary agent, send a similar letter, asking if they would be prepared to handle your book. Better still, of course, would be a personal introduction, because the chances of receiving a favourable reply from an agent, unfortunately, are likely to be even fewer than from a publisher. But, if you're writing to one or two agents, wait to hear from them before you approach any publishers.

Finally, remember that both publishers and agents are in business to make money and are not philanthropic institutions. Unless one of them believes your book has a chance of achieving reasonable sales (a minimum print run is usually three thousand), they will probably turn it down. Literary agents earn their living by taking a percentage (usually ten per cent, but occasionally higher) from whatever you make from your book. Agents will generally look after your interests (because they coincide with their own), negotiating as high an advance as possible, maybe selling foreign rights and ensuring your contract is a fair one. Thus, if you are lucky enough to find one willing to handle your book, it may well be to your advantage.

PRESENTATION

If you intend to submit your book to a publisher, or excerpts of it in the form of articles to feature editors, you *must* present it correctly, if for no other reason than to prove you have a professional approach.

- Type in double-spacing (not single or 1 ½) using size A4 paper, on one side only, leaving a minimum of 1 ¼ " all round. *Never* submit hand-written work.
- Use a new ribbon and replace when worn (don't test editors' eyesight – it won't improve their temper or make them more disposed to consider your MS favourably).
- Number pages consecutively throughout. Chapters should not be numbered separately.
- Check that spelling and grammar are correct.
- Don't start common nouns with a capital letter. For example: company, uncle (unless used as a title: Uncle John), postman, town hall, hotel.
- Keep a copy of your MS for your own file in case the original is lost.
- Don't put the pages of a full-length MS into any kind of binder (editors hate them). Secure with an elastic band and place either in an empty typing-paper box (ideal for the purpose) or in a large reinforced envelope. Articles can be stapled or paper-clipped.
- Always enclose either a stamped-addressed envelope or stamps to cover return postage. It is also useful to include a stamped and self-addressed postcard for acknowledgement of safe arrival of a full-length work.
- Include a cover sheet with both short and long MS on which you state your name, address and telephone number, pseudonym if you've used one, title of work, approximate number of words (to nearest 100 for a short piece, nearest 1000 for a book) and date. For an article, add the words First British Serial Rights, which merely

means you are offering the editor the opportunity to print your piece for the first time in the UK and are retaining your copyright.

- If you are submitting a full-length autobiography to a publisher, you will have previously sent a query letter to which you have received a favourable reply, inviting you to send it in. In this case, a short covering letter, addressed to that editor by name, is sensible. In the case of an article, a covering letter is not really necessary.
- *Never* send the same article to more than one publication at the same time. Neither is it wise (quite apart from being very expensive) to submit a full-length MS to more than one publisher/literary agent, at the same time (known as multiple submission). Although this practice is becoming more common in the US, it is still discouraged in the UK. If you do wish to submit your book (not article) to several publishers, simultaneously, it is only courteous to tell them you have done so.
- A final word of warning: *never* turn up at a publisher's offices to enquire about your MS. If you haven't heard from them (or from a magazine editor) within three months, a polite letter of enquiry is acceptable.

Word count

There is a simple effective method to calculate the number of words in your typescript which is as follows:

- Count the number of words in 25 *full-length* lines, then divide that total by 25 to find the average number of words per line. For example, 292 words divided by 25 equals 11.6 words per line.
- Count the number of lines per page (normally, this should be the same on each) and multiply by the figure arrived at (i.e 11.6). Thus, 30 lines multiplied by 11.6 equals 348 words per page.

- Count the number of pages in your typescript and multiply by the number of words per page. For example, 221 pages multiplied by 348 words equals 76,908 words, approximately 77,000 words.

LIFE BEGINS AT ANY TIME

by

AUDREY B. NOBLE-SMITH

Autobiography/article submitted by:
Mrs Audrey B. Noble-Smith,
22, Carlton Drive,
Westingham,
Cheshire CH24 HB2
Tel: XXXXXXXXXX
Length: Approx 65,000/1500 words
[First British Serial Rights for article only]
Date:

SELF-PUBLISHING

If your ambition is to see your life story in book form but you can't find a bona fide publisher to take it, what then? One possibility is self-publishing – but it is the route to go only if you have the stamina and determination to undertake all the work involved: editing, proof-reading, finding a typesetter (or negotiating a price with a small independent firm), designing a book-jacket, registering it for an International Standard Book Number (ISBN), without which it will not be eligible for Public Lending Right (PLR), arranging for it to be reviewed by newspapers and magazines and, last but by no means least, marketing the finished product.

It *can* be done, as David Atkins (with the one hundred per cent support and help of his wife) proved with his autobiographical account of his wartime experiences in Burma called *The Reluctant Major*, an extract from which will be found in Section 6. It even ran to a second edition and fully paid for itself – but they were experienced business people and knew how to deal with the myriad problems that can often arise (including, in this case, arriving back from holiday to find a thousand copies of the book waiting practically on their doorstep!).

There are two possible viable alternatives to undertaking self-publishing on this scale. One is to find a small (preferably local) printer or book producer (there are now a number of these around since the proliferation of new technology) and obtain a quote for however many copies you want of a simply-produced book. Also ask to see examples of their work before signing a contract. At the time of preparing this typescript, I obtained quotes, for a small run of a shortish book (100 – 140 pages) in a single-colour paperback cover, in order to give some indication of likely cost. Working on an average of 350 words per page, these were as follows:
A 100-page book: 25 copies – £185; 50 – £265; 100 – £395
A 140-page book: 25 copies – £245; 50 – £320; 100 – £455

On top of these figures, there would be a charge for typesetting in the region of £3 per page and, if editing was also required, there would be a fee for that, also.

The second alternative is to have it neatly typed (worth paying a professional typist if you're not too good at it, yourself), and getting a small local printer to photocopy and bind as many copies as you want. This would be considerably cheaper though, of course, the result would be less attractive to the eye.

Finally, a word of warning. Despite the many blandishments and promises of vanity (or subsidy) publishers, who frequently advertise in the press as being publishers seeking new authors, resist them. It will prove extremely expensive (*you* have to bear all the costs of production, regardless of anything suggested to the contrary) and little or no marketing will be undertaken. This is because, basically, few shops will sell vanity-published books unless, perhaps, they are by a local author when they might be persuaded to take a few copies on a 'sale or return' basis.

From examples I have seen, they are often poorly edited (or not edited at all) so that grammatical and spelling errors remain uncorrected, the result too often being a sadly substandard book.

It is far better to see your life story produced in the simplest possible form at no very great cost than to spend possibly thousands of pounds and be left with a huge surplus of books which nobody wants.

Paula Atkins (wife of the author of *The Reluctant Major*) describes how, in 1985, after her husband had unsuccesfully tried to interest several publishers in his book, and at the suggestion of a publishing friend, they decided to 'have a go' at doing it themselves:

> After *The Reluctant Major* had plopped through the letter box for the seventh time, accompanied by yet another polite letter of rejection, we decided to publish it ourselves with the help of our friend's ungrudging advice.

139

There are two stages in the process of self-publishing: there is the actual production of the book and, second – even more difficult – its promotion and sale.

The first stage involves a bewildering period of decision-making – choosing the typeface and format for the text, design of jacket, selection of publication date, price and so on and, above all, choosing the right people to help.

The typesetter, recommended by our friend, helped us lay out the work in the script of our choice and explained the many difficulties involved in finding the least expensive way of doing it.

The publication date must be decided early on in the proceedings to ensure that the finished bound books will be ready eight weeks before publication, thus allowing time for reviews; and at least three months before publication, applications must be made to the Standard Book Numbering Agency for an International Standard Book Number. Without this official recognition, the book will not be included in *British Books in Print*, the 'bible' of libraries and bookshops. A finished copy of the book must be sent to the Copyright Office of the British Library; thus ensuring inclusion in the British National Bibliography.

Acknowledgements, contents page, list of plates and so on had to be juggled with but, even so, we ended up with six wasted pages.

The next big hurdle was the jacket – but here a delightful young friend of the family, a Chelsea art student not yet qualified, came to our aid and created a cartoon illustration for the front cover which undoubtedly encouraged sales.

Working closely with the artist, the typesetter laid out the text for the front and back covers, a photographer prepared a picture of the author and a fourth person put everything together and produced a jacket in two colours of the size in frequent use in libraries.

This was the moment when scrupulous checking had to be made on grammar, punctuation and spelling as changing camera-ready copy is very expensive and not to be undertaken lightly.

Like building a house, a book has to be put out to contractors and the number of people involved had, by then, risen to eight. We had run up a total cost of £2700 for one thousand copies on good-quality paper with hardback cloth binding, sixteen first-class plates and 600 spare jackets for publicity purposes.

In order to cover costs and make even a small profit, we knew we would have to sell at least 500 copies at a price of a little over £5. The figure of £7.95 was finally decided upon and included on the jacket flap before the final copy was approved.

However, the real struggle – the second stage – had yet to start. To help pass the nervous waiting period, we took a holiday and arrived home to find a thousand books on the doorstep! In fear and trembling we tore open one of the parcels and, to our enormous relief, the books appeared as good as we could have hoped.

We were pleasantly surprised and very excited when *The Reluctant Major* was extremely well reviewed in two national papers and given wide coverage in our county of Sussex. We spent several days visiting all bookshops within a radius of fifteen miles and leaving copies on a 'sale or return' basis.

After nine months hard but enjoyable work, we had covered publication costs and scheduled a second print-run, but what a lot there had been to learn and hurdle after hurdle to overcome before the book passed from typescript into the finished product. But, by the time the last copy of the first edition had left the house, another thousand copies had been ordered.

DIY publishing undoubtedly costs a lot of money but there is enormous added satisfaction of giving birth to your own 'baby'.

Since the publication of this first book, David Atkins has

written and published two more, the latest being *The Cuckoo in June*. *Tales of a Sussex Orchard*, about their life as apple-growers in Sussex, extracts from which are scheduled to be broadcast on BBC Radio 4 in 1993. Copies of *The Reluctant Major* and *The Cuckoo in June* are available from The Toat Press, Tullens Moat, Pulborough, Sussex RH20 1DA.

Examples of autobiographical writing

INCIDENT IN IRAN BY JEAN WADDELL

On May Day, 1980, I hit the headlines. Unknown to me, as I floated in and out of consciousness in a Tehran hospital bed, attached to various drips and tubes, the UK tabloids were screaming: 'Scottish missionary shot in Iran'.

Normally, that day, I would have wakened up in Isfahan where, for three and a half years, I had been secretary to the Bishop in Iran. Looking forward to returning to the UK for a break, my heart had sunk when my exit visa was refused. A couple of lines in Arabic script, which had mysteriously appeared in my passport, were translated by the bearded official as 'The holder cannot leave Iran without special permission'.

Having exhausted all possibilities of help in Isfahan, I had fled to the British Embassy in Tehran. Although under great pressure because of the volatile political situation in post-revolutionary Iran, they suggested I stay in the capital for a few days while they tried to sort out the problem. Which explains why, that May morning in 1980, I had woken up in a small flat on the top floor of our Diocesan Centre in Tehran.

Although my exit visa had been refused, I didn't feel

143

personally threatened until, at about eight-thirty that morning, I opened my door, porridge pot in hand, and stared down the barrels of two guns. One of the fierce-looking young men brandishing them said, 'We are revolutionary guards and we want to question you.'

I couldn't believe this was happening but, stifling a gasp of fright and steadying my trembling knees, I tried to appear calm and confident. Resisting their efforts to push me into my kitchen, I suggested, 'Why not come into the sitting-room – have some coffee – put away your guns. I'm quite happy to answer your questions.' They agreed and one sat down, gun out of sight, while his companion prowled around the flat, picking things up and showing them to the other.

During the next half-hour, I was subjected to a barrage of questions. Why was I still in Iran? Why hadn't I left with the other Westerners? What was I doing here?

After explaining about my work with the Bishop and the Episcopal Church in the whole of the Middle East, I felt I had convinced them that I was no threat to the revolution. They didn't agree and insisted they must blindfold me and take me to their headquarters. One moved behind me but, instead of blindfolding me, he hooked his arm around my neck, jerking me off my feet, which the other grabbed. As the arm gripping my throat tightened, I struggled for breath and began sliding into unconsciousness. The thunder and fireworks display in my head almost drowned out my fleeting prayer, 'O God, I didn't expect it to be so soon, and certainly not in this way, but here I come.'

A large hand came down for another blow. A voice in my head seemed to whisper, 'Relax!' I went limp and knew no more until I found myself on my bed, bathed in what I thought to be sweat, and gasped, 'Gosh, what a nightmare!'

But it wasn't. My hands and feet were tied, my left side felt too heavy to move and the 'sweat' was really blood because, although not aware of it at the time, I had been shot while lying there, lifeless. In one of my lucid moments, I managed to free my hands and feet. I struggled to raise myself to get to the telephone, which was out of reach, but my body refused to obey my efforts. Later, I realised how fortunate this was because any such move could have proved fatal as I would have lost more blood more quickly.

© Jean Waddell

Jean was rescued by a large, friendly policeman and her life saved by an Iranian surgeon, whose own life was subsequently threatened for doing so. Subsequently she was imprisoned in Tehran for seven months until her release was effected by Terry Waite, the first time the Archbishop of Canterbury's personal envoy at the time was involved in rescuing a hostage from the Middle East. Despite her ordeal, Jean retains a great love of the Iranian people.

Comments Jean Waddell has led an unusually interesting life, with many years spent living and working for the Church in the Middle East, the strong thread running through it being her faith in God. When planning her autobiography, it was decided to open with the dramatic and traumatic incident, which was to be the biggest test of her faith, in order to engage the reader's attention, immediately. Once that had been effected, she would then go back to her childhood where, on the sands of her home town in the north-east of Scotland, her interest in things religious was kindled through listening to the Salvation Army band on Sunday mornings and which also led to her love of music. Her story would then continue, chronologically, until it reached the incident in Iran, the result of which closed that fascinating chapter of her life in the Middle East.

This piece demonstrates the effectiveness of choosing a high point in your life to start your autobiography and attract your reader's interest, setting the tone of what is to follow.

EXTRACT FROM *THE RELUCTANT MAJOR.* BY DAVID ATKINS

I did not want to be promoted to major, I did not want to leave the exciting life of a young staff captain in Delhi, a city I loved with its shady tree-lined streets. In Delhi, for me, there was hunting in the crisp dawn of the Indian winter, tennis at the Club and every party was bright with the pretty daughters of senior officers. No, I did not want to leave Delhi, but I was kicked firmly out and upstairs.

While I was a staff captain I had made two big mistakes. There were no calculators in those days, and with my chartered accountant's training I had been given the job of working out the Indian Army's food requirements for the next two years. While doing this a slip in a decimal point in the rum calculation resulted in an over-order for ten times the amount of rum the Army needed. The Indian Army was planned to go up in size by ten times from 200,000 to 2,000,000, but with my mistake the increase in rum ordered was one hundred times. All over India rum-makers received staggering orders from GHQ (India), put everything into maximum production and started making rum like mad. It was in fact a mistake that was to prove very valuable to the Army.

My other mistake was that I placed all the Army's reserve stocks of atta into Karachi. Atta is the coarse ground flour used for the flat chappatti. This is the unleavened bread of the Bible and was the main food of the sepoys from the north of India. At the time I had a logical reason for sending everything to Karachi – the main theatre of war for the Indian Army was the Middle East, and the flour was grown chiefly in the Punjab. It seemed reasonable to stock it on the west coast of India which was much closer to the war than Bombay or Calcutta. Everything moved so fast in that expanding army that I never discussed my action with any senior officer, so thousands of tons of bagged coarse flour were bought all over central and northern India and trundled

146

week after week along the various railways with their changing narrow and broad gauges, across the Sind Desert to Karachi high up on the west coast. Soon the Karachi depot bulged with food all ready for shipping to Egypt, and then the Japanese war started.

As troops were hurried out to Malaya and Singapore, atta was urgently needed there from Calcutta or at least from Bombay. It was not there; I had put it all in Karachi. It was not possible to move the flour back by rail across India because of the varying sizes of the railway tracks and so the flour had to be moved around the bottom of India by chartered ship.

The brunt of General Wavell's displeasure fell on the Quartermaster General but the man who finally carried the can was Lt.-Col. Wally Watts, a plump and pear-shaped officer with a good temper and an untidy uniform. He was a man of great efficiency who never got the recognition he deserved for keeping two million soldiers fed and supplied.

I bore him no grudge for deciding that I must go. I had done very well in my previous job in Poona but in General Headquarters in Delhi, at the age of twenty-three, I never really related the orders which went out from our small office to what was actually happening around India and further afield – I could not visualise their full effect. Later I was often on the receiving end of staff orders which had not been clearly thought out; they came from senior officers but quite possibly originated from young captains. It is hard to get such orders changed, and if one tries to do so, it does not help one's own reputation. Wavell writes: 'The feeling between regimental officer and the staff officer is as old as the history of fighting.'
©David Atkins

Comments This extract is close to the opening of the author's autobiographical account of this part of his life, during the Second World War. That first sentence, in fact, would have been an effective opening for the book itself.

David Atkins has deliberately chosen to relate in an amusing style the story of his two potentially disastrous mistakes as a young army officer in India, in the early part of the war, and their results. It provides a fascinating glimpse into army life, at that time and in that place, which will surely bring a smile to the lips of many and a wry, reflective nod from others.

EXTRACT FROM *NO ONE SPECIAL* BY DOREEN STEPHENS

One evening, towards the end of 1952, Jack came in from the surgery carrying an article he'd read in the *Evening Standard*, written by George Campey, its Broadcasting and Television correspondent (he later became the BBC Television Press Officer). Television was growing fast and the BBC, some months before, had decided they should advertise for an editor to provide women's afternoon programmes on television, similar to 'Woman's Hour' on radio. (BBC-TV had recently been set up as an independent branch of the BBC, answerable directly to the Director General, at that time, Sir George Barnes). The Television Talks Department, under Mary Adams, was already running two women's programmes each week but had decided they needed an editor to take charge, if they were to be developed. George Campey, short of a news story, had decided to tease. 'They seek her here, they seek her there!' he headed the article in which he asked what was happening, it then being nine months since the advertisement for the position had appeared.

'There you are,' Jack said, handing me the cutting. 'There's your career!'

I laughed and told him not to be so silly – but I read it, none the less.

It did not go away. It kept turning up when I thought it was entirely in the waste-paper basket. Three nights later, with the dinner cooked and awaiting Jack's return from evening surgery, there, catching my eye, was the article. Waiting on Jack's return was always unsettling. It could be two minutes or, if he had a last-minute call, two hours, or anything in between. Suddenly, I thought, 'I'll amuse myself and draft a letter of application for that BBC job.' When it was written, I was surprised it looked so good. I decided to type it, together with a CV and, finally, an envelope. A few minutes later, Jack came bustling in.

'There's that letter to the Beeb you've been trying to make me write,' I greeted him. 'If you want to send it, you can put a stamp on it,' I added rather ungraciously as I went into the kitchen to fetch the dinner.

He pushed his glasses to the top of his head, read the letter carefully, got out his pen, inserted two commas and proceeded to fold it, put it in the envelope, stamp it, went to the front door and along to the postbox on the corner, all without a word!

Some months later, after sundry interviews with Leslie Page, Head of Television Establishment, Cecil McGivern, the Controller of Television Programmes, and Mary Adams, Head of Television Talks, I was summoned to an Establishment board meeting, complete, in those days, with a Civil Service Commissioner. This was followed by a polite letter from Leslie Page, thanking me for attending and asking me not to accept any other offer of employment without first letting them know.

Days, weeks, a couple of months passed. The summer holiday period was supposedly an excuse for the delay. When we were well in September, I had had enough. I sent a polite letter asking for a decision, one way or the other, as I needed to plan my autumn schedule, if I was not to be offered the job as Editor of Television Women's Programmes. It resulted in an immediate telephone call of apology and a promise of a quick decision, which arrived by letter, a few days later.

I was invited to present myself at Alexandra Palace on Monday, 26 October – the day after my forty-first birthday

– to start my duties at a salary of one thousand pounds per
annum – big money in those days. I clearly remember
excitedly setting off to work, that first morning, in my
ancient, secondhand Daimler, high off the road with a foot-
board, and arriving at Alexandra Palace, entering by the
Tower entrance and taking the lift to the sixth floor.

I had two weeks to familiarise myself with the production
routine, get to know my two producers, S. E. Reynolds, a
long-time BBC Sound Producer who was providing a weekly
practical programme called 'About The Home', and
Jacqueline Kennish, who produced a general interest
programme called 'Leisure and Pleasure'. I also met the
hostesses of the two programmes, Joan Gilbert and Jeanne
Heale.

I listened, questioned, watched and waited. But my
survival was, in large measure, due to S. E. Reynolds – SE,
as he was affectionately known by all who worked with him.
An old and experienced radio producer, wise in the ways of
the Beeb, he decided to accept me, taking me under his
protective wing, tactfully guiding me and saving me from
making any gross blunders. We became good working
colleagues, sharing a mutual respect for each other plus, on
my side a deep sense of gratitude for his unselfish generosity
to me, in those early days.
©Doreen Stephens

Doreen Stephens was editor of the BBC's afternoon women's
programmes, then became head of children's programmes
before, eventually, leaving to join David Frost, at his
personal request, to help start up London Weekend.

Comments The author of this piece had had a fairly
unexceptional life until she was almost forty years of age. At
a time when many women were beginning to feel the need to
be more than 'just housewives', a coincidence set her on the
road to a career in the early days of TV, one for which it
might be said she had no particular qualifications.

The style is a simple, straightforward narrative, interspersed with occasional bits of dialogue and with some of those 'brush strokes' that let us see her husband, Jack, reading through that vital letter of application and herself, driving to work on that first day at Alexandra Palace.

Doreen Stephens's autobiography will surely provide a valuable insight into that period when TV was in its infancy and although, as her title suggests, she might not have been anyone special, she proves the point that 'she matters'.

WHEN I WAS A CHILD BY AGNES ORANGE

I had a happy and unusual childhood. My father was a corporal in the Royal Garrison Artillery, No 1 Mountain Battery, serving on the Indian North-West Frontier, and I was born in the Rawalpindi Station Family Hospital on 5th March 1912.

The first eight years of my life were spent moving from station to station with my parents. Winter was spent in Quetta, Rawalpindi or Peshawar, moving to the Murree Hills for the summer. This meant packing up our home every six months. The trunks and household goods were despatched by camels or mules. The women and children travelled by *dandi*, a type of sedan chair carried by coolies. Sometimes, part of the journey was made by train.

The families were always accompanied by a military escort. We stopped overnight at a dak bungalow (a purpose-built hut-like building). Mother always took a picnic basket, water, primus stove, kettle, toilet necessities and potty on all journeys.

On arrival, families were allocated quarters, furnished with a table, chairs, bed-irons and bedding that had to be stuffed with coirhair (from coconut) to make mattresses, and a rifle-rack and kitbox for the soldiers.

As I was a very timid child, the Medical Officer encouraged me to ride a donkey. A safety-saddle and donkey were purchased and riding lessons began. The confidence test came when we were going to a Regimental Sports Day. To reach the sports field, a wide ditch had to be crossed. A temporary bridge had been construted over this *nullah*, but the donkey stubbornly refused to cross it. Suddenly, he took a flying leap across. My parents were horrified but relieved when I yelled, 'Daddy, tell him to do it again!' On leaving the sports, the obstinate creature refused to jump and, this time, calmly crossed the bridge.

In 1917, my father was promoted to Quartermaster-Sergeant and posted to Quetta. The climate was such that we were able to stay the whole year, although the summer was very hot and the winter extremely cold. I saw snow for the first time!

At Quetta, I went to my first native bazaar. The memory of it remains with me to this day. The seething mass of people had to be seen to be believed. The blind, deformed beggars at the gates, near-naked fakirs, fortune-tellers casting their forecasts in the sand, snake-charmers, scribes and groups of men smoking their hookahs, women wearing colourful saris, proud Afghan tribesmen going about their business. The bazaar was a hotbed of gossip and rumour. Intelligence agents – Indian or British soldiers in disguise – gathered vital information about uprisings and planned raids. We never went alone: a trusted bearer always escorted us.

Quetta, being a large military station, had a school. It was quite a distance from our bungalow so I travelled there by bullock-cart. Instead of a whip, the driver used a heavy stick with a nail in the top which he plunged into the bullock's rump. It upset me so much that, one day, I knocked his turban off. This caused an awful commotion.

The following winter, father's battery was posted back to Rawalpindi where news came of a dangerous uprising on the Afghan border. The regiment moved out to try to contain it, leaving a detachment of troops to guard the station and families. Orders were given that, if an alarm sounded, all families should go to the Sergeant's Mess for safety. My sister and I were put to bed as usual; Mother packed an emergency bag and rested, fully dressed. Maroons sounded the alarm early in the morning. A soldier arrived to take us to the Sergeant's Mess where we were barricaded in. The smaller children were bedded down on the billiard tables. All the windows were blacked-out and only a hurricane lamp gave light. Prayers were said for the regiment's safe return, which were swiftly answered. The emergency ended and we returned to our quarters before sundown.

In February 1921, Father was posted back to England. We sailed from Bombay on Troopship *Brandenburgh* and arrived at Southampton on 7th March. My Indian childhood was over.

Published in *Woman's Weekly*, January 1992, and reprinted here by kind permission of the Editor.

Comments   The simple narrative style of this extract from Agnes Orange's autobiography is in keeping with the relating, from a child's perspective, certain incidents in what was a very unusual childhood. It allows us a glimpse into a way of life vanished forever – that of the British Raj.

A good deal of ground is covered in less than a thousand words with many small but fascinating descriptive details included. We are given a brief pen-picture of what it was like for the families of men serving in the Indian Army on the North-West Frontier, early this century. We have a child's eye view of a native bazaar, of the landscape both on the plains and in the hills and how mothers coped with potentially dangerous emergencies in such surroundings.

EXCERPTS FROM *LIVING WITH TERMINAL CANCER* BY DR ROBERT SHEPHERD

Diet for one, you can eat what you like. I adore eggs in any form – fried, boiled, scrambled, shirred, eggs Benedict, devilled, in aspic, in Hollandaise sauce – you name it, I pick it, except that current fads have kept me down to a one-egg-a-day ritual until the day before yesterday when the CAT-scan printed out: 'This man can eat all the eggs he wants.' It was a kind thought mixed in among other more Presbyterian announcements on the wages of sin and the need to repent without delay.

It included cheese also, of course, from the tangy Jarlsbergs and Emmentals to the sharp cheddars and provolones, and on to the creamy Bries, Neuchâtels or – heaven help us! – a fine warm Stilton spread thickly on a Carr water wafer. Just imagine what you are missing, all you permanent people.

You have to Fight Back, Whether you want to or not!

Time to meditate more, pray more, waiting on the divine process to unfold as it will. Time to love more and be loved more by those who could not or would not (yourself included) let love and grace flow over and around you, uplifting, healing, moving on.

So you cry together and laugh together and yearn for more, even while knowing that mourning starts the day you are born, and ends only when the gut releases memory at last. The text-books say mourning takes from six months to a year, but that's nonsense; it takes longer than that, sometimes forever.

What I mean is people who die suddenly miss a lot of all this, including the chance to mourn each day a little as you go along.

But there are negatives to terminal cancer too, clearly.

You soon discover, for example, that cancer is a collective illness and not a private matter as you had surmised at the start. People feel free to call at any hour of the day or night, inquiring how you are, or to visit without notice, bearing gifts, examining you carefully on arrival. They say: 'You look better than I thought you would,' making you feel vaguely guilty and suggesting the judicious use of eyeshadow for the next time. Since dying is heavily into theatre, you have to look your part.

Many people ask how you are and then tell you in some detail how they are, or how their great aunt vanquished terminal cancer by prayer, or a guided meditation, or baby wheat ground up and stuffed with anchovies into garlic buds four times a day. Guaranteed! She lived to 102 and ran under a moving bus thinking it was stationary.

Call a Spade a Spade

And don't mince words while you're at it, call a spade a spade.

It's a bugger, that's what it is. Dying is the shits.

Write About It

After you've talked about it, write about it, get it down on paper. Writing helps crystallize thought, bringing into focus what you intuit way down but can't see clearly on the surface. Remember the old tag line: How do I know what I think until I've read what I've written?

Write letters to friends, keep a diary, write articles for publication. Many papers and magazines are open to first-person accounts of serious illness and how people cope with it, and pay you for it to boot. If you make some money out of this misery, why not try?

. . . the thing wrote itself, flowing out of the pain and fear, out of the doubt and despair, and gradually out of the joy and understanding that have grown from looking at this horror not only as a tragedy in my life, but as an opportunity to find meaning and acceptance through it.

If you've tried it before, try it now. Writing is one of the highest forms of therapy.

Psychiatrist Robert Shepherd died on 29 September 1990, part-way through writing this series of articles.

Derek Cassel, editor of *The Medical Post*, a Canadian medical journal, has kindly given permission for these extracts to be included in this book, saying that they had never before had such an overwhelming response to any article or series and that Dr Shepherd's work had touched many, many readers very deeply indeed. He added that he believed Bob Shepherd would have approved of their being used in this way.

Comments   When I was given a copy of the special issues of *The Medical Post* containing Robert Shepherd's account of living with terminal cancer, I felt both awed and moved. I could only admire the courage of this man, a doctor himself, thus knowing the truth about his illness and its implications, who was able to write about it to help others in the same situation.

   If we are truthful in our writing, inevitably, we expose something of our thoughts and deepest feelings but, here, the author openly discusses his fears, his efforts to come to terms with his fatal illness and, most importantly, how to *live* with it, getting the most out of his remaining time with family and friends. Incredibly, he also manages to relate all this with a touch of humour.

EXTRACT FROM *ASANTE MAMSAHIB* BY EDITH CORY-KING

My malaria came once a year, for certain. Twice, said my parents, was acceptable but regularly recurring bouts could be proof of a pernicious variety or a sign that the parasites had retreated to inaccessible parts to weaken the body and place it at death's door. When I fell victim to the latter condition, Papi once more went to buy drugs from the hospital. But, as the weeks passed and the malaria struck frequently, though without a perceivable pattern, the preparations of quinine appeared to be as ineffectual as his promises to reduce weight by eating less.

Papi said we had to consult another medical opinion. He had heard of a Mission doctor who had saved Africans regarded as incurable by the Government Hospital. He would leave a letter with a *duka* from which the Mission bought its provisions. Missions, I thought, were the homes of those religious white people mistakenly trying to stop blacks from behaving according to their tribal customs. Papi had made jokes to that effect.

Mutti said that blacks from Missions behaved like slaves, servile, repeating their greetings like a dirge and bowing and curtseying like dolls on strings. She preferred not to have a Christian house-boy, especially if he was going to refuse to wear the Mohammedan-style white cap or fez.

When an answering note invited us to attend the Lutheran Mission, I was too weak to care where we were going. The sun rose to heat the day. Our lorry, laden with cases of petrol because there would be none available at our destination, a basket of food and bread and fruit for the driver and his *turni-boi*, churned up the dust of the track in a rolling cloud behind us. On three sides, the savannah stretched to the horizon, on the fourth, low hills were faintly visible in the distance. Yellow grass, dried thorn bushes, acacias and giant baobab trees, thick in girth and almost devoid of leaf, were indicative of the season's arid conditions.

Mutti, I knew, was trying to make me feel better by exclaiming every time we sighted something moving, 'Look Puzi! What lovely antelopes, there, under the umbrella tree.' 'Oh, you must see this. Quick, have a look. What an ugly lot! Vultures, probably eating something dead near that baobab.'

At last, we came upon the Mission built of grey stone, as was the church and its spire, standing among tall trees. A door opened and a nun beckoned us to enter a cold, echoing room, then led us to another room where a bearded man greeted us from behind a desk laden with books and papers. It was not long before the consultation was finished and I heard him say, 'Promise me you will try.'

157

'Yes, yes,' Mutti answered in a tone I knew meant, 'Never!'

At the bottom of the escarpment, on the return journey, back in the shimmering heat, faint billows of smoke hung in the steaming sky. Omari pointed a stubbled chin in their direction. '*Moto!*' Relentlessly our track veered towards what we all knew was a bush fire raging ahead of us.

Mutti glanced anxiously at him. Omari ignored her and looked ahead with studied indifference. We might have been approaching a rain-cloud. From afar, swirling smoke and leaping flames made passage through them look impossible. As we approached where the fire had already been, smouldering tussocks radiated enough heat to bake bread. Stumps of bushes and thorn trees were still alight and birds circled aimlessly in eddies of hot air, having lost their nests.

I was very frightened, the more so at the thought of the remaining tins of petrol on the lorry. The moment we entered the fire zone, Omari turned his head to sound a warning through the back window and depressed the accelerator to the floorboards with his big flat foot. The engine leapt forward, adding its roar to the inferno of crackling and exploding flames, and the lorry careered at breakneck speed to beat the elements.

It swayed alarmingly, threatening to go off course into the fire. Mutti clasped me tightly as though the bolted door might open to shoot us into the open mouth of the fire dragons. It was terrifying: the proximity of an uncontrolled fire, the heat of the air making it difficult to breathe, the smoke obliterating the road and, lastly, the sight of an antelope racing panic-stricken alongside the lorry, threatening to cross the track in front of us, made me want to cry. On the other hand, the moment was too exciting for tears!

On our arrival home, Papi asked Omari why he had not waited for the fire to pass on before taking the lorry through its heat.

'Waiting would have delayed us until late,' he replied. 'That would have been bad for the *mtoto*.'

As for the consultation, the doctor had told Mutti about a drug called Esanofeles, recently perfected in Italy.

'What did you have to pay?' Papi asked.

'Nothing. Hans, absolutely nothing. He would not accept a cent.'

My father looked relieved. 'Very nice of him because I expect this Esanofeles will be expensive.'

In due course, it expelled my parasites and my malaria reverted to the two-a-year variety.

©Edith Cory-King

Comments Once again, this is an account of a quite exceptional childhood. There have been many autobiographies and novels, depicting white colonial life in Africa before the last war, but this one, I think, is unique. Edith Cory-King was of German/Austrian parentage, frequently living in primitive conditions and with only Africans for neighbours and companions so that German and Swahili were her everyday languages. English was a completely foreign tongue to her until she was sent to a boarding-school where she was forced to learn to speak it.

A graphic and descriptive account of the difficulties and dangers of life in the bush, effectively told from a child's viewpoint, builds up to the climax of a terrifying but exciting incident. Yet even this pales into insignificance compared with the grinding, ever-present lack of money with which to maintain just a basic way of life for a cultured European family in Africa, between the wars.

DON QUIXOTE BY PHYLLIDA MORISON

That donkey was a character: a 'card', our Cockney factotum, Revell, used to say. He had been a 'Tommy' in the First World War, washed up and somehow stranded in Paris. He and Donkey-Oatey got on well together. They had the same sort of impudence and the same kind of bad temper.

They both relished tobacco and it amused Revell that the donkey prised cigarette packets out of his pocket and chewed them and that he liked to eat whole tablets of soap. It was frightening to see him frothing at the mouth and blowing huge bubbles out of his nostrils, but Revell always kept his coat shining and his hoofs bright.

My father took no notice of the donkey, except to photograph him, and to insist that we must pronounce his name 'Donchiote', in approximation to the Spanish – not Don Quicks-oat. We comprised with Donkey-Oatey – it seemed appropriate.

This beautiful beast with his neat carriage was a source of acute embarrassment to the older girls. Only twenty minutes from Paris and a donkey! Other people had cars and we had a donkey! It was not to be borne, and they never mentioned him to their friends at the Lycée, and lived in dread of being seen out with him. We younger chldren were overjoyed, though. A splendid vehicle was available for picnics and the donkey was an excellent ride, swift and sure-footed.

My strong-willed, determined mother didn't care a button what anybody thought. With upwards of twelve people to feed, she needed a conveyance for market and Donkey-Oatey was always ready. Tuesdays from Chatou, Fridays from Le Vesinet, the little cart would come back loaded with the most enormous bundles of delicious food.

Unfortunately, this delightful creature was *'entier'*, as the dealer told my mother when she bought him. He was also very young and very randy. Possibly, too, we fed him too many oats. My mother, however, had some strange idea that, when we were out with him or our big, curly-haired sheep-dog, Meess, we were safe. I think her hair would have turned grey very quickly if she had known of some of our adventures.

One of Donkey-Oatey's habits was to try and climb walls when he heard the braying of an attractive-sounding Jenny on the other side. At least once he tipped the cart up completely on its end and dislodged the three of us, me and my two little sisters, depositing us with all our picnic paraphernalia, books and swimming gear, on the road. It was quite difficult to untangle the harness, get him out from between the upright shafts and re-harness him. Meanwhile, someone from the other side of the wall had removed the Jenny and we were able to reorganise things and go on our way. (We were en route for the banks of the Seine in the direction of St Germain, where we would swim between the barges in the most filthy water imaginable. It must have been very much like swimming in a sewer.)

Cats must chase mice, dogs cats – and Donkey-Oatey women on bicycles. For some obscure reason, the sight of a woman pedalling away would excite him to a frenzy and give him an unbelievable turn of speed. We put him into blinkers to restrict his side view but, if he caught a glimpse of a cyclist in front of him, *nothing* would hold him back. He would pound away at full gallop, especially if he could get on to the tram-lines which then ran between Le Pecq and St Germain. I remember standing up and trying to rein him in while a frightened woman pedalled away for all she was worth, glancing back from time to time in terror. If he finally caught up, he would nip her smartly in the rear and once he tweaked a mouthful of fabric out of a light, flowered dress. Had not two people stepped forward and stopped him, I don't know what would have happened next. I remember conflicting feelings of fear and embarrassment and pride, too, at being something like Jehu on a flying chariot. I don't know why we were never arrested.

©Phyllida Morrison

Part of an article entitled 'Donkey-Oatey', published in *The Lady*, March 1992.

Comments   A personal experience with a difference. From the opening sentence, we know we are to be entertained, made to laugh as the author introduces Don Quixote, the colourful 'main character' of the story and describes some of his more outrageous habits. It is hardly surprising that this delightful vignette of somewhat Bohemian family life in the suburbs of Paris was accepted for publication, immediately.

THE DAY THE RSM'S HOUSE DIDN'T BURN DOWN BY BILL AXWORTHY

To my left, 600 tall, black Askari, in immaculate khaki uniforms, stood steady in the Kenya sun. The basic khaki was relieved only by their blue puttees and cummerbunds and red fezzes. Their faces were impassive, the dark skin marked with tribal scars and, here and there, a Kipsigis had the split lobes of his ears hanging down almost to shoulder level. In front of me was the back of the CO and, beyond him, the empty saluting dais with the camp a white maze behind.

A green staff-car drew up at the edge of the parade ground and a tall figure in a red-banded hat emerged and climbed the steps to the dais. The Brigade Commander had arrived. Behind him, four of his staff officers sorted themselves out and stood, still and silent, in a short rank.

'Battalion,' the CO roared. We stiffened. 'Battalion – Attention!' 600 pairs of feet hammered the ground. 'Slope Arms.' The Askari adopted the position with three sharp, accurate movements of their rifles. We waited. Finally, the Annual Administrative Inspection of the 5th Battalion of the King's African Rifles began.

The King's African Rifles was a locally recruited regiment commanded by British officers and NCOs. The Askari were carefully selected from the many volunteers and represented all the tribes of Kenya except the Kikuyu who had not been regarded as trustworthy since the Mau-Mau troubles, earlier. They were smart and, by African standards, reliable soldiers.

The day's events were always ushered in by a ceremonial parade of the entire battalion, which included a detailed inspection, and culminated in a march past the inspecting

162

officer. Afterwards, all the officers and the inspecting Staff retired to the officers' mess for the one item of the programme which gave the battalion a chance to hit back at the Staff, getting as much alcohol into them as possible so they would be unable to carry out the afternoon's inspection of the battalion's books and accounts with any degree of thoroughness. Sometimes it worked, sometimes it didn't, but it was worth a try.

On this occasion, all went well until the entire party, accompanied by the CO, the Regimental Serjeant Major and myself, the Adjutant, were strolling towards the mess. We reached the RSM's quarter, which was situated on the main road through the camp and surrounded by a six-foot-deep monsoon ditch, the only access being over a narrow foot bridge. The Brigadier paused, then turned to the CO and said, 'The RSM's house is on fire! Do something about it.'

The CO, never at a loss, looked at me. 'Fire in the RSM's house, Bill.' I thought this a bit unfair but recovered my wits and turned to the RSM. 'Fire in your house, RSM. Sound the alarm and get the fire trailer.'

The RSM doubled to the nearest telephone. There then ensued one of those awful silences. The Brigadier admired the playing fields. The Staff officers gazed about them, admiring the back of the camp's telephone exchange. The CO looked anxiously at the camp road, down which the fire trailer would come. The RSM's wife, attracted by the unusual crowd of officers, stuck her head out of the kitchen window. I just prayed.

The minutes dragged past until the RSM sidled up to me and said out of the corner of his mouth, 'Bloody fire trailer's got a puncture. The MT's serjeant's fixing it. Sir,' he added.

Immediately, the fire-alarm sounded with an ear-splitting shriek. It was mounted on the telephone exchange and further conversation was impossible, for a few minutes. As it whimpered into silence, a Land Rover swung out of the MT yard and hurtled towards us, towing the fire trailer which was swaying dangerously on one nearly flat tyre, then pulled up with a flourish as the pump crew of excited Askari jumped out of the back.

I won't go into the detail of what happened next but the salient points were as follows. We couldn't get the fire trailer over the monsoon ditch around the RSM's house. When we did, it wouldn't start. When it started, we found we didn't have enough hose. When we found enough hose, it sprang leaks along its entire length. And we lost the nozzle.

The Brigadier's face was frozen in disbelief. One of the Staff Officers was nearly hysterical with laughter and the RSM's wife had a clearly audible fit of giggles.

It was a thoughtful party that continued to the officer's mess and the afternoon's inspection of the books was the most thorough we had ever experienced.

The CO left, shortly afterwards, and the new CO appointed another officer as adjutant. I often wondered whether it had anything to do with the day the RSM's house didn't burn down.

©Bill Axworthy

Comments With this extract from a retired Major's autobiography, we are quickly informed of the where, when, what and who of the episode being related. The story is neatly told in an unforced humorous style with just enough detail to allow us to 'see' the setting in which the events took place.

EXTRACT FROM *I'D DO IT ALL AGAIN* BY KIT PETERS

Whilst rehearing at the 'Ally Pally', we had been all the time with our troupe of dancers, now [at the start of touring] we were meeting more of the cast. Not the 'stars', they travelled separately, but some who made up the cast of *Humpty Dumpty*.

We were fascinated by the whisky-drinking men, playing poker and smoking endlessly. The carriage became fog-bound with Players' Weights' smoke and the smell of alcohol. We were to learn, later, even this was highly favourable to what we discovered behind the door on which we knocked so gingerly in Liverpool's Lord Nelson Street – a dingy street full of small, ugly, terraced houses, mostly theatrical digs, for that was the way these poor souls made their living.

When the door was opened, we came face to face with·a fearsome landlady. Hair in curlers, she was wiping her red-raw chilblained hands on a none-too-clean apron, her staring eyes of liquid blue scared me into believing I was meeting a character straight from the pages of Dracula.

A shiver ran down my spine as she opened her thick lips to bellow, 'Well, don't stand there a-gawping. Come on in.'

The stench of fish and stale cabbage-water made me gulp, fearful of throwing up, as I followed her up the narrow, dingy staircase to the attic bedroom which was to be ours.

'There y'are – and lucky to git it this time of year.' I stared in disbelief, not knowing such awful places existed, as she went on to say, 'Your sittin' room's downstairs, the lavvie's through the kitchen owt back. And, by the way . . .' She emphasised by wagging a filthy finger. 'Don't you let me a-catch you going owt there on the ole man's baffnight, cos 'eel be in his nothins in the kitchen, see. That's on Friday nights.'

'Haven't you got a bathroom, then?' I enquired, meekly.

'A baffroom?' she guffawed, throwing back her greasy head of curlers. 'No, I bloody ain't, Miss La de da. A baffroom!' she repeated. 'What, for twelve and a bloody tanner a week? Come orf it.' And, with that, she tut-tutted down the stairs, calling back. 'Yer tea'll be ready in five ticks.'

©Kit Peters

Comments The scene of cheap theatrical digs and the horror they arouse in the two young women, finding themselves staying in them for the first time, is deftly painted, in this fascinating piece of autobiography. The stench of fish and stale cabbage-water, the landlady's greasy hair in curlers and her none-too-clean apron, together with the superbly-written, totally in character dialogue, all help bring the setting and situation to life for the reader.

EXTRACT FROM *THE SANDS OF TIME* BY LILIAN GARNER

The bringing down of the great tin trunk from the attic was our signal for preparations to begin for our annual summer holiday. This trunk would be packed, locked and roped. The carrier, with his great shire horse, would come to collect it, sending it on its way to await our arrival at the lovely little town of Tighnabruaich.

It was a place my father loved, a place where he and his brothers had spent most of their boyhood. We grew to love it, too, and were always eager to return there. For us, it was a time of discarding our white needlework petticoats, knickers and buttoned-boots of those Edwardian days, days when we would be allowed the freedom of being scantily-clad, a time when, in my memory, the sun always seemed to shine.

In 1900, my father had come to England to manage an iron foundry in the north-west and the holiday for him would be a welcome break from the heavy, exacting and sometimes dangerous work: to mother, a relief from the dust and dirt, for our house was built on the foundry site.

The journey was another part of our delight. We travelled by train to Manchester, then by cab across the city to Victoria Station for the train to Glasgow and then another train to Wemyss Bay. Then we boarded the steamer *The Mercury* (though we could never understand why it sounded like 'Marycary' when the local people said it).

Another excitement was the sail down the Clyde and tea

on the boat – Scottish teabread, an assortment of little scones, shortbread and pancakes dripping with butter. We never lingered over this, being all impatience to get on deck to catch the first glimpse of the pier in the place we all loved, with the friendly hills beyond, looking down.

We raced ahead of mother and father to Corran Cottage, with its outside stone stairway leading to the upper floor, its windows overlooking the sea, small rooms and beds in the wall.

This was the only time in our young lives when the word 'don't' was little used and, soon, my brother and I were running down to the shore. Here, I first learned to love the sea and know it in all its moods. It was a somewhat rocky shore with pebbles sharp on our feet, but a treasure-house of starfish, sea-urchins, crabs and other creatures in the rock-pools.

Tired of swimming and beachcombing or watching the porpoises in the bay, we would wander down to the pier whenever a boat came in or to the boatyard to watch the men at work. They never seemed to mind us getting in their way and good-naturedly answered our many questions.

Mother and father visited friends or relatives during the daytime but, most nights, went out deep-sea fishing for our meals, next day. One day, we persuaded father to row us across to the island where we could have a picnic. Mother packed the basket and, heavily laden, we set out, father's powerful strokes taking us swiftly across the bay.

Our first task on landing was to gather sticks for the fire to boil a kettle while mother laid the cloth and set out the food. Looking up, we saw a great bull on the hilltop. 'Is he dangerous?' we asked.

'Certainly not,' said father. 'Sit down and get on with your tea.'

We had barely started when, with a tremendous roar, down he came. We were flung pell-mell into the boat, father the last to leap in, with the bull following, loudly bellowing his anger at this invasion of his territory. On he came until the water was too deep then, returning to the shore, he stamped our picnic into the ground, throwing the turf back over his head. At a safe distance, we watched, still trembling to think what might have happened to us if the sea had not let us escape. I have never, knowingly, walked in a field with a bull in it ever since.

We were allowed to visit the tiny shop which sold everything, from stamps, postcards and sweets to paraffin oil. We spent our pennies on candy and coconut ice and other home-made sweets, then lingered near the shore to watch the graceful yacht, *Iolaire* (The Eagle) come sailing into the bay and remind ourselves to look for her after darkness fell when she would be lit up like a fairy palace. She would be the last thing we would see as we set off on our return home.

Tearfully, we parted with most of our collections of treasures from the shore, there being a limit to what the trunk would hold, and sadly we waved goodbye to friendly faces. In 1914, the war came and put an end to our Scottish holidays.

©Lilian Garner

Lilian Garner has written her autobiography for her family who urged her to put down on paper the story of her life.

Comments An Edwardian childhood and a summer holiday of nearly ninety years ago are vividly evoked, in this piece, through the many tiny details of travel, of teatime and of simple holiday pastimes. Describing an era long since past, which obviously remains clear in the author's memory, she cleverly builds up to a climax with the incident of the appearance of the bull during a picnic, concluding with the start of the Great War and the end of an idyll.

EXTRACT FROM *AN AUSTRALIAN CHILDHOOD* BY DIANNE MORRIS

Sometimes I think of the Heinbergs. They were a family of about ten, always a baby slung on one of their hips, and Mr Heinberg either away droving or in clink for drunken brawling. But they stuck together. Mrs Heinberg would march down to the police station, baby bawling on her hip, and shout abuse at whichever officer was on duty. The children, mostly boys except for the three girls who were around my age, were famous for fighting, and you could never win a fight with a Heinberg because, sooner or later, a sister or brother would join in and help.

The day they confronted me outside the Post Office gave me my first taste of the Heinberg style. Animal cunning, sarcastic, one for all and all for one. They even spoke together in sing-song, taunting and mocking. When they laughed at me, I felt angry and humiliated but powerless. They, on the other hand, were rough and powerful. If you weren't careful, they would hit you, bite you, scratch at your face, hurt you with their sly tongues, and stick together against you. If only my mother had broken their spell with anger. But all she said was, 'Sticks and stones will break your bones but names will never hurt you.' And yet she was angry – so angry that she was almost spitting when she got home and told Nan.

What I felt most angry about, at the time, was them picking on my purse [it was her seventh birthday and the purse was a present]. Perhaps my purse was my armour which they dashed to pieces with one thrust of their cruel little tongues.

Was it a sort of Heinberg overture of friendship? If it was, I wasn't up to the challenge, not against three of them. They were probably acting as a corporate body, the only way they knew how. But, deep inside me is still pain and resentment and mixed feelings about that encounter. Do I want to now dash them with my superiority? Show off my education, clothes, upper-middle-class kids with 'Pommy' accents?

I imagine, now, they're all drovers' wives, themselves, knowing hardship, hunger and poverty, as well as all the ills associated with poverty. I see them barefooted, ugly from wear, dried up, pinch-faced with matted hair, despair written on their faces, surrounded by kids they batter as easily as swatting flies. They have poor command of language, speak with harsh voices and live in shanties. But, still, I think of my revenge. I want to add my own personal triumph over that of their fate.
©Dianne Morris

Comments The style of writing in this piece of autobiography is particularly noteworthy, the words and phrases clearly having been chosen with care to create the desired atmosphere of fear, hostility, anger and resentment. Drunken brawling, baby bawling, shouted abuse, animal cunning, sharp and sarcastic, sly tongues, cruel tongues. Re-read the last paragraph and see how much information we are given in just a few sentences. And the final sentence which sums up how the author has never forgotten, nor fully forgiven, those children for ruining her seventh birthday.

SECTION SEVEN

Information

REFERENCE BOOKS FOR WRITERS

A Dictionary of Modern English Usage by H. W. Fowler, OUP, 1965

First Steps in Family History by Eve McLaughlin, Countryside Books, 1989

How to Write and Sell Your Personal Experiences by Lois Duncan, Writer's Digest Books (available from Freelance Press Services, Cumberland House, Lissadel Street, Salford, Manchester M6 6GG)

1000 Markets for Freelance Writers by Robert Palmer, Piatkus, 1993

Research for Writers by Ann Hoffman, A. and C. Black, 1986

Shorter Oxford English Dictionary

The Fiction Writers' Handbook by Nancy Smith, Piatkus, 1991

The Realities of Fiction by Nancy Hale, Macmillan, 1963

Thesaurus of English Words and Phrases, P. M. Roget, Penguin.

The Writers and Artists' Year Book (annual), A. and C. Black

The Writer's Handbook (annual), Macmillan/PEN

Tracing Your Ancestors in the Public Record Office by Jane Cox and Timothy Padfield, HMSO, London 1985

Trace Your Family History by L. G. Pine, Teach Yourself Books, Hodder and Stoughton, 1984

USEFUL PUBLICATIONS (FOR WRITERS GENERALLY)

Directory of Writers' Circles by Jill Dick, available from: Oldacre, Horderns Park Road, Chapel-en-le-Frith, Derbyshire SK12 6SY

Family Tree Magazine, 15/16 Highlode, Stocking Fen Road, Ramsey, Huntingdon, Cambridgeshire PE17 1RB.

Flair For Words Newsletter, 5 Delavall Walk, Eastbourne, Sussex BN23 6ER

Freelance Writing and Photography, Tregeraint House, Zennor, St Ives, Cornwall TR26 3DB

Quartos, BCM-Writer, 27 Old Gloucester Street, London WC1N 3XX

Writers' Monthly, 29 Turnpike Lane, London N8 0EP

Writers' News, PO Box 4, Nairn IV12 4HU

USEFUL ADDRESSES

Creative writing courses/conferences, etc:
Write Your Life Story, et al, tutor Nancy Smith, at Dillington House, Ilminster, Somerset TA19 9DT tel: 0460 52427

Creative writing in France, details from:
LSG, 201 Main Street, Thornton, Leicestershire LE6 1AH tel: 0509 231713

The Arvon Foundation (held in Devon and Yorkshire), details from:
Totleigh Barton, Sheepwash, Devon EX21 5NS

Age Exchange Reminiscence Centre, 11 Blackheath Village, London SE3 9LA tel: 081 318 9105

Dynix Library Systems, Quay South, Salamander Quay, Park Lane, Harefield, Middlesex UB9 6NY tel: 0895 824091

Flair for Words, details from 5 Delavall Walk, Eastbourne, Sussex BN23 6ER

The Book Partnership, Redmays House, Cheddar Road, Wedmore, Somerset BS28 4EP tel: 0934 712345

The Hen House (women only), North Thoresby, Lincolnshire DN36 5QL

Writers' Holiday, Administrator, Anne Hobbs, 30 Pant Road, Newport, Gwent (annually in July)

Writers' Summer School, Hon Sec, Philippa Boland, The Red House, Mardens Hill, Crowborough, Sussex TN6 1XN (annually in August)

SOME AUTOBIOGRAPHIES FOR SUGGESTED READING

A Child in the Forest by Winifred Foley, BBC/Futura
An Immaculate Mistake by Paul Bailey, Bloomsbury/ Penguin
A World Apart by Daphne Rae, Lutterworth
Beyond the Nursery Window by Ruth Plant, Kimber
Boy – Tales of Childhood by Roald Dahl, Cape/Puffin
Castaway by Lucy Irvine, Gollancz
Diana's Story by Deric Longden, Bantam/Corgi Books
Emma and I by Sheila Hocken, Sphere Books
Hovel in the Hills by Elizabeth West, Faber & Faber/Corgi Books
Not Quite Heaven by Brenda Courtie, SPCK
Not Without My Daugher by Betty Mahmoody, Corgi Books
Policeman's Patch by Harry Cole, Firecrest, Chivers Press
Somewhere a Cat is Waiting by Derek Tangye, Michael Joseph/Sphere Books
The Forest Trilogy by Winifred Foley, OUP

The Hills is Lonely, et al, by Lillian Beckwith, Hutchinson
The Past is Myself by Christabel Bielenberg, Bantam Press
The Year of the Cornflake by Faith Addis, Andre Deutsch
They Must Have Seen Me Coming by Louise Brindley, Cassell/Futura
They Tied a Label on My Coat by Hilda Hollingsworth, Virago
Twopence to Cross the Mersey by Helen Forrester, Cape/Fontana
Waiting in the Wings by Doreen Tovey, Michael Joseph

Piatkus Books

If you enjoyed this book, you may be interested in reading other books on writing and journalism published by Piatkus. For a free brochure with further information on our complete range of titles, please write to:

Piatkus Books
Freepost 7 (WD 4505)
London W1E 4EZ

PIATKUS

The Fiction Writers' Handbook
Nancy Smith

The Fiction Writers' Handbook is an essential guide
and reference book for everyone who wants to
write a novel or short stories. This comprehensive
volume is packed with detailed advice and practical
information on:

- The techniques and principles used in all
  fiction writing – including characterisation,
  dialogue, theme, conflict, pace and flashback

- The novel and its construction

- The short story and how to find a market for
  it

- Working methods, synopses and presentation

- How to get your work published.

*Nancy Smith has taught creative writing for over
12 years. She has written short stories, articles,
a novel and a non-fiction writing guide,*
The Essential A-Z of Creative Writing.

1000 Markets for Freelance Writers
Robert Palmer

Freelance writers want to be sure of placing their work quickly for the maximum financial reward. What they really need is a reference book which will target those magazines and journals which are likely to take their articles.

1000 Markets for Freelance Writers is the first freelance writers' handbook uniquely geared towards the demands of the typical freelance writer. Comprehensive, up-to-date and meticulously researched, it identifies the thousand most genuine and lucrative market opportunities and includes:

- An easy-to-use A-Z listing of the best freelance markets

- A directory cross-referenced by subject

- Advice on approaching magazine editors and preparing articles

- Guidelines on rates of payment

With profitable outlets for your work becoming more and more difficult to find each year, *1000 Markets for Freelance Writers* will be an invaluable addition to every freelance writer's bookshelf.

How to Make Money from Freelance Writing
Andrew Crofts

How to Make Money from Freelance Writing is the essential book for everyone who has ever wanted to write for a living but didn't know how to do it in a professional way. It will show you:

- How to get started

- What to write about

- How to sell what you've written

- How to get commissioned

- How to interview people

- How to overcome blocks and barriers

How to Make Money from Freelance Writing is packed with advice on all areas of writing – fiction, short stories, travel, newspaper and magazine journalism, TV and radio scripts, interviewing and ghostwriting. Whether you are a new or published writer, this practical guide will show you how to make more money from your writing skills.

'A very useful, totally practical guide' ... *Daily Mail*